Y0-DPC-838

Discarded by
Santa Maria Library

The Good Years

Snippets of Santa Maria Valley History

by Shirley Contreras

for the Santa Maria Valley Historical Society

THE GOOD YEARS
by Shirley Contreras
Copyright ©2001
by the Santa Maria Valley Historical Society
616 South Broadway
Santa Maria, California

All rights reserved. No part of this book may be used or reproduced in any manner whatsoever without written permission except in the case of brief quotations embodied in critical articles and reviews.

On the cover: Looking north at the 200 block of South Broadway, this photo was taken in the early 1950s from the upper story of the Sousa Building, then the location of Sears & Roebuck. At left, across the alley from the Grayson Hotel, can be seen the classic façade of the Santa Maria Theater, and, north of the Church Street intersection, the B&B Coffee Shop. Beyond Main Street stands the old Bank of Santa Maria building; on the east side of Broadway, north of the Texaco station, can be seen the sign for Bowers & Stokes, the local Ford dealer.

Designed by Richard Cole, Graphics LTD
Santa Maria, California

Printed in the United States of America
ISBN: 0-9714389-0-0

*This book is respectfully dedicated
to all of the pioneers
of the Santa Maria Valley—
past, present and future.*

MANY THANKS TO THE PEOPLE who so willingly shared their family's histories, personal memories, photos and expertise, thus enabling these few chapters of the valley's history to be enjoyed by those who come after them.

Special thanks to the many pioneers who have so graciously given me the help and encouragement with which to write my weekly column for the *Santa Maria Times*. With deepest thanks, I share the authorship with all of the above, as, without them, I could write nothing.

In addition, thanks are extended to the *Santa Maria Times* for permitting some of my columns to be incorporated into this book.

I hope that you will enjoy these few stories that tell a bit of the history of our beautiful valley.

Everyone must recognize the fact that recollections, and even sources, are not infallible. Therefore, the Santa Maria Valley Historical Society must hold itself not responsible for errors which may have crept into this book.

*Shirley Contreras
Santa Maria, Calif.
August 30, 2001*

About the Author

■ SHIRLEY (KELLY) CONTRERAS was born and raised in Westford, Massachusetts, graduated from Westford Academy (the second oldest academy in the United States), and pursued many careers, most of which entailed writing.

She moved to California in 1963, and, while raising three sons, she worked in both the Civil Service and private sectors.

In 1991 she moved to the Central Coast, where she had the good fortune of meeting some of the finest people in the world. She considers the friends that she's made in the Santa Maria Valley as family and the Central Coast as her home.

She began writing "The Good Years" column for the *Santa Maria Times* in 1991 at the suggestion of Marilyn Cronk, who was then serving as curator at the Santa Maria Valley Historical Museum. She has voiced unending thanks to the many fine people who were willing to share their family's history as well as to the editors at the *Santa Maria Times*.

Special thanks go to Richard Cole of Graphics LTD in Santa Maria for the help that he's given in the layout of this book. His expertise in design is second to none.

Many thanks to those who contributed financial assistance for the publication of this book.

PLATINUM
Mr. and Mrs. Joe Olivera
Santa Maria Valley Chamber of Commerce
Mr. R. H. Tesene

GOLD
Adam Brothers Farming, Inc.
Mid-State Bank
Vandenberg Federal Credit Union

SILVER
Ms. Laura Abeloe
Dr. and Mrs. Harold Case
Mr. and Mrs. Richard Chenoweth
InWest Insurance Services
Dr. and Mrs. Bruce Howard
Judge and Mrs. Royce Lewellen
Los Padres Bank
Mr. and Mrs. Douglas Mussell
Mr. and Mrs. Douglas Reeves
Ms. Elizabeth Scott
Ms. Ann Visscher

Table of Contents

William Foxen's Branding Iron

ILLIAM BENJAMIN FOXEN, destined to play a major part in the colorful history of the Central Coast, was born in Norfolk County, England, in 1796. As a young boy, he went to sea, first with the British Navy and later with the British Merchant Service, where he earned the rank of First Officer.

After resigning from the Merchant Service in 1815, he purchased a schooner and set sail for the islands of the Pacific. Two years later, while his ship was docked at the Sandwich Islands (Hawaii), he met Captain A. B. Thompson, who took him on as First Officer of his hide and tallow trade ship, which was sailing between California and Boston.

A few years later, Foxen went into the same business for himself, using his own ship to work between Mazatlán, Sinaloa, the Sandwich Islands, Yerba Buena (San Francisco), the port of Monterey and San Diego. He made his first visit to Santa Barbara in 1818.

He eventually gave up the sea, sold his boat and opened a general merchandise store in Santa Barbara.

Sometime in the late 1820's Foxen met Eduarda del Carmen Osuna, daughter of José María Eugenio and María Antonia Marta (Cota y Lugo) Osuna, and stepdaughter of José Tomás Antonio Olivera. After his satisfying the church's requirement that he convert to Catholicism, the couple was married at the Mission Santa Barbara on May 26, 1831.

In May of 1837, Foxen was granted the 8,874-acre Rancho Tinaquaic, where he eventually built an adobe ranch house, along with structures to protect his animals.

Out of necessity, rancheros were self-sufficient. Nearly every necessary commodity was made on the premises. Foxen's soap, made from ashes of a special bush in Tulare, was considered to be the finest in the area. In addition to his harness shop, he had a blacksmith shop, where he made his ranch implements, including a branding iron in the shape of an anchor.

Hard times for the Foxens came after Fremont and his army of soldiers came through the area on their way to Santa Barbara in December of 1846. Foxen's young son, Guillermo, led the men through the San Marcos Pass to Santa Barbara, where they captured the town without bloodshed

ILLUSTRATION BY RICHARD COLE

on the 27th of December.

Californianos, feeling that Foxen was a traitor to his adopted country, raided his rancho, set fire to his fields and torched his house. Fearing for his family's safety, he took his wife and children to live at the Santa Inés Mission, eventually moving them to the ranch of his godfather, Daniel Hill, where they remained until he felt that it was safe to return to the ranch.

Once back on the ranch, Foxen continued with his ranch operations; his stock increased and his financial picture continued to improve. Shortly before he passed away in 1874, he divided the rancho among his eleven surviving children.

With descendants of Benjamin Foxen now numbering in the thousands in California, it's little wonder that the whereabouts of the man's cattle brand might have been unknown.

No one seems to know why it wound up at the Converse Ranch in Santa Paula. After the Foxen relic was uncovered during the digging of a trench in 1904, the Converse family held onto it for 20 years before donating it to the Ventura County Museum of History and Art. Although it's not clear if the family knew of the history of the branding iron, the Museum officials did.

It was a mere coincidence that during a special Museum exhibit in 1924, Gerald Foxen saw his grandfather's branding iron on display.

Benjamin Foxen's distinctive brand, forged and registered in 1837, is in the shape of an anchor with an off-center circle at the top. Foxen chose the anchor in commemoration of his days at sea.

When a special Ranchos exhibit was scheduled to be held at the Santa Maria Valley Historical Museum in June of 1991, Richard McCartney, a great-grandson of Benjamin Foxen, felt that the exhibit could not be complete without his ancestor's distinctive branding iron being a part of the exhibit. Knowing that the iron was then in storage at the Ventura Museum, McCartney and Marilyn Cronk, the Santa Maria Museum curator, began negotiations to borrow the iron for the occasion.

It was a great day for the Foxen family when McCartney arrived at the Santa Maria Museum carrying the famous brand in his hands. On hand to meet him were three of Foxen's great-grandchildren, Winston Wickenden, Inez Goodchild and Leon Wickenden, as well as Richard Dore, a great-great grandson.

Feeling that the distinctive branding iron was more a part of Santa Maria Valley history than that of Ventura County, McCartney and Mrs. Cronk began a campaign to keep the iron at the Santa Maria site permanently. After much negotiating between the two museums, the Ventura officials finally agreed to let the brand stay in Santa Maria.

Through the efforts of a few, the distinctive relic of a man who was one of the valley's first rancho grantees was brought to the Santa Maria Valley Historical Museum in 1991, 87 years after it was unearthed many miles from its origin. &

Juan Pacífico Ontiveros

UAN PACÍFICO ONTIVEROS was no stranger to the Central Coast area when he and his wife, Martina, acquired the Rancho Tepusquet in 1856. The area was cattle country, with few ranchero homes, no towns and no roads. El Camino Real was merely a trail leading from mission to mission.

Since there were so few Spanish people living in California during the earlier mission era, they all not only knew each other, but became inter-related through the marriages of their children and grandchildren.

Juan Pacífico, the eldest son of Juan Patricio and María Antonia Rodríguez y Noriega Ontiveros, was born in Los Angeles on September 24, 1795. He followed in the footsteps of both his father and grandfather by enlisting in the Spanish Army in 1814, serving for about 20 years.

Although it's not clear why Juan Pacífico decided to leave his southern California property (now the cities of Placentia, Fullerton, Brea and Anaheim) and purchase the Rancho Tepusquet, he did

have family connections there. Martina's sister Eduarda, the wife of Benjamin Foxen, lived on the nearby Rancho Tinaquaic.

Juan Pacífico and María Martina del Carmen Osuna, daughter of José María Eugenio Osuna and María Antonia Marta Cota y Lugo (and stepdaughter of José Tomás Antonio Olivera), were married in November of 1825 at the San Gabriel Mission. The couple settled on the Rancho Santa Gertrudes, where the first of their many children was born.

In June of 1856, Juan Pacífico and his sons drove 1200 head of cattle from their property in southern California to their newly acquired Tepusquet property and proceeded to build an adobe home in a recess at the mouth of the Santa Maria Canyon, completing it in 1858.

Although Rancho Tepusquet was isolated, life followed the usual rancho pattern. At first deer were plentiful, but they soon retreated up into the mountains. Coyotes and grizzlies, often preying

Juan Pacífico and María Martina Ontiveros

on the calves, soon became bold enough to take the cattle right out of their corrals.

According to his son Abraham, after California became part of the United States in 1850, Juan Pacífico kept from 15 to 30 thousand cattle on hand at his ranchos, selling them to drovers who showed up at different times throughout the year. The prices, varying according to the season, ranged from $15 to $35 a head.

The arrival of a buyer signaled the start of the rodeo. Both the ranchero's and drover's vaqueros began by rounding up 5,000 cattle and then started the process of cutting out the fat three- and four-year-olds to be turned over to the buyer. Payment was always made on the spot in gold, sometimes in $20 gold pieces, and at other times in six-sided $50 slugs put out by San Francisco firms and stamped with their name to make sure of the weight and fineness of the gold. Those special slugs were called *estranjera* ("something strange"). The drovers, preyed upon by such notorious *bandidos* as Jack Powers and Salomon Pico, carried their money in belts wrapped around their waists and under their clothes.

After California became a state in 1850, the rancheros not only changed their nationalities, but had to learn a new language, new laws, new customs and new ways of doing business. Juan Pacífico was born a Spanish subject, later became a Mexican citizen, and, at the age of 55, became an American.

In keeping with the Spanish tradition of celebrating one's patron saint's feast day, Ontiveros always threw a party on the 23rd of June, the feast day of San Juan. His 8-day party consisted of the usual feasting, drinking and dancing throughout the day and night, and catching just enough sleep to get ready for more of the same.

The most famous fiesta of all took place in 1872, when Juan Pacífico suggested to John Thomas Goodchild, "You have the sheep and I have the cattle. Let us ask all the other 'Juans' in the valley to celebrate our saint's day." All seven of the Juans—Juan Pacífico Ontiveros, Juan Nicolás Ontiveros, Juan Pedro Olivera, Juan Flores, Juan B. Ruiz, Juan de la Cruz Ruiz, and Goodchild— got together and gave the biggest fiesta that the valley had ever seen. *Ramadas* (shelters for the dancers with roofs made of branches) were built on the Tepusquet Ranch, and women brought their stoves to use in barbecuing the meat.

With the women in *carreteras* and the men on horseback, those traveling to the fiesta could only cover from 10 to 15 miles per day. Those who came from distances as far away as Los Angeles camped out at night or stayed at convenient *rancherías* along the way. People began to pour into the ranch the day before the scheduled event, and spent the next three days dancing to fiddle music when they weren't eating and drinking.

Land title problems seemed to plague Ontiveros. Some he won, while others he lost, one of the last being a dispute with Juana Mariana Olivera over her interest in the Rancho Tepusquet. He lost the case, and in March of 1875 he paid a sum of $2750 to Juana Mariana, her second husband Francisco Villa, and William J. Graves.

The Olivera lawsuit took its toll on Juan Pacífico's health, and he didn't live long enough afterwards to enjoy what old deeds called "peaceful and undisturbed possession" of his property. He died on March 7, 1877, at the age of 81 years, and is buried in the San Ramón Cemetery, the third burial there. His wife, Martina, an invalid for many years, died 20 years later.

Mary Long Rice

ARY LONG, one of twelve children, was born in Ross County, Ohio, on June 24, 1836. A tomboy at heart, she became an expert horsewoman and was certainly not afraid of hard work. Although it's not clear when her family moved to Missouri, that's where Mary began her education in a one-room school, so typical of the times.

In 1853, when Mary was 17 years old, she joined her family in an oxen-drawn prairie schooner train headed for California. To insure an adequate food supply, the travelers drove a herd of cattle, with Mary, expert horsewoman that she was, helping to care for the herd during the trip westward. Since the cattle had to live off the land, the trip was slow.

The tediousness of the trip west was broken up by the many adventures that the group encountered on its journey through Indian country. The family became uneasy when Mary's father refused an Indian chief's offer of six choice ponies in exchange for his daughter. When the marriage refusal brought no reprisals, everyone breathed easier.

While the wagon train was camped at Bear River, Idaho, an old Indian woman sat fishing from a log which had fallen across the river. When a 15-year old boy from another wagon took out his rifle and shot the woman, her lifeless body fell into the river.

The next day a large band of angry Indians rode into the camp demanding that the boy who had killed the squaw be handed over to them. The horrified people watched as the Indians took the boy from his hiding place, crossed the river to the other shore, and burned him alive. Satisfied that justice had been done, the Indians left.

With up to twelve oxen to a wagon, when it was time to camp for the night, the group would form a circle for protection and place the cattle in the middle, hoping to keep the animals from straying or being stolen.

Six months after leaving Missouri, the Long family arrived in Healdsburg, California, where Mary met 17-year-old John Henry Rice, who had come west by mule train in 1849 in search of gold. Like many other Argonauts before him, Rice found disappointment in the gold fields and decided to go into farming.

After Mary and John were married in 1854, they moved to Sonoma County, where Susan, William and Dover were born. In 1867 they moved to Salinas, where they farmed for another six years.

In 1873, when William was seventeen years old, the Rice family moved to the Santa Maria Valley. The family settled on leased property west of town, and later purchased a portion of the old Punta de la Laguna Rancho near Guadalupe.

When the Rice family had made enough money from crops to pay off the loan on the property, young William, carrying the gold, took a stagecoach to San Francisco. Although stagecoach robberies were common at the time, both William and the gold arrived safely.

Life in those early days was difficult. Mary's day began at 2:00 a.m., when she prepared breakfast for the men who hauled grain to schooners from the valley to Point Sal. In addition to her regular chores of cooking at the fireplace, baking, washing, and making clothes, she wasn't above joining the men in building and repairing fences.

Mary did more traveling than did most women of her time. In addition to accompanying her husband when he visited his family in Tennessee, she also made several trips to San Francisco by steamship.

Mary rode her horse sidesaddle, as did all proper women of her day. She could handle a gun or fishing rod as well anyone, and she passed her love of hunting and fishing on to her children. William vividly remembered his mother placing a muzzle-loader in his hands when he was only nine years old. The boy confidently rested the heavy weapon on a fence rail and bagged his first wild duck.

When Grandma Rice was 61 years old, her husband died. Although she could have lived with her children, who were then well established in business and ranching, she opted to stay in her own home at 715 South Lincoln Street. Her schedule of rising early every morning to take care of her chores never deviated. She drank three cups of coffee a day and, in spite of her hearing loss and partial loss of eyesight, she remained in good health.

The high-spirited Grandma Rice was a hard worker right up to the end. As she often told her family, "I have never faced anything which made me want to quit!"

Although she had not been ill, Grandma Rice passed away on June 16, 1936, just eight days short of her 100th birthday. In the words of her son, she was just "worn out."

Stagecoaches on the Central Coast

ONCORD STAGECOACHES were virtually indestructible, and breakdowns were a rarity. The familiar oval-shaped hardwood body's interior contained leather upholstered seats just big enough to seat three passengers each. The jump seat in the middle could seat three additional passengers. However, since the seat was hard and the dirt roads were rough, the passengers experienced a trip that was both memorable and uncomfortable.

The driver, usually controlling six horses or mules, sat on the outside right front, elevated from the level of his passengers, while the all-important Wells Fargo box sat underneath him in a space sheltered by curtained leather. If the contents of the box were determined to be of particular value, an armed guard rode shotgun.

"Mudwagons," with doors and windows removed to reduce weight, were used to ride through the rocky mountain roads.

A stage coach driver was one of a sturdy breed of men capable of controlling six lines with which to lead his horses. With the lines laced between his fingers, he controlled one or all six horses at the same time. The driver, or "jehu," was the boss, and his team knew it.

The driver's whip was a symbol of his proud calling. It was both the tool of his trade and the badge of honor of his rugged profession. Whips were never sold, borrowed, or traded.

The Arellanes adobe in Guadalupe served as one of the earliest stagecoach stops in 1861, as did the Foxen and Wickenden adobes and Ballard's station.

The night hours were especially hazardous times to travel by stage. Even though two lanterns were attached over the front wheelers, they didn't provide much light. With rough roads and sometimes no visibility, especially during rainy weather, drivers had to rely on the horses to get them over the rough roads.

Stage stops were a convenient distance apart, the distance a six-horse team could travel at a full gallop (about 15 miles), depending on the terrain. Routes varied through the years. In 1867 there was a stage station at the Suey Crossing of Santa Maria and later at La Graciosa.

At an earlier period, the stage route followed the Santa Maria River and went south through

Foxen Canyon to the stagecoach station at Benjamin Foxen's adobe.

During John Waugh's time, no guards were on board, and a 40-mile run over the San Marcos Pass from Mattei's Tavern to Santa Barbara took about six hours. In case of robbery, drivers were instructed not to put up any resistance. When the robber demanded, "Put 'em up! Throw off the box," the driver did as he was told.

As time went by, the stagecoach routes changed. However, with the coming of the narrow gauge railroad from San Luis Obispo to Los Olivos in 1886, stage traffic ended between those two points. Then, in 1901, when "The Gap" was closed, allowing through rail service between Los Angeles and San Francisco, the stagecoach era came to an end as the much-coveted mail contracts were shifted from stagecoaches to the railroad.

Tommy Hicks, Dave Shean, Selin Carrillo, "Whispering George" Cooper, Joe "Fat" Cropper, Burt Wheelis, Johnny Waugh, John Coleman, Sam Butterfield, Tom Edgar, Charlie Patterson, "Uncle George" Heller, Tom Cole, Harry Cook, Charlie Jennings, Frank Cook, Wesley Froom,

and James T. McCrosky were but a few of the colorful drivers who rolled along the stagecoach routes in Santa Barbara County.

Celeste Robasciotti came to California in the 1880s from Gordola in the Canton Tocino in Switzerland. He lived in Guadalupe, where, in addition to doing some dairy farming in the area, he drove a stage line between Pismo Beach and Guadalupe. The stage line ran from Guadalupe through Oso Flaco and along the beaches to Pismo.

According to his great-grandson, John Robasciotti, one day while the man was driving his team, a canoe in the water spooked the horses and the stage tipped over. With the stage ruined, Robasciotti was without a job, and the area was without service until the coach could be replaced.

Robasciotti continued operating his dairy farm until he contracted valley fever. Since the notorious Guadalupe wind and dust caused his condition to worsen, his doctor advised him to return to Switzerland, where fresh air would clear his lungs. Robasciotti returned to Switzerland where both his health and finances improved, and, although he never returned to the United States, his children came and settled in the Soledad area.

The LeRoy Bros. and Rancho Guadalupe

N IMPORTANT CHAPTER in the history of the Rancho Guadalupe, one that was destined to affect its future, began when Theodore LeRoy passed away in San Francisco in 1882. He had acquired title to the great rancho through foreclosure in the 1870s, had subdivided and sold some of the land, yet he had never set foot on the property.

Within a period of thirteen years the Rancho Guadalupe had passed through the hands of the original grantees, Teodoro Arellanes and Diego Olivera; Antonio Arellanes; the Estudillo family; and finally, Theodore LeRoy.

It took ten years to complete the complicated probate. When the LeRoy estate was finally distributed, one half of the property went to Theodore's brother, Victor, and one quarter each went to Victor's sons Eugene and Georges. Victor transferred his one-half interest to Rene de Tocqueville, the husband of his daughter, Henriette.

Since none of the LeRoy family had ever seen its newly acquired property, Eugene and Georges sailed from San Francisco to Port Harford on a small schooner, which stopped at every port on its way south. From Port Harford they rode in a creaky buckboard over the bumpy 30-mile road to Guadalupe.

After arriving in the town, the two brothers stayed at the Grisingher Hotel. Although the hotel rooms were partitioned off, the makeshift walls reached only part way to the ceiling. There was, of course, no plumbing, only a bowl and pitcher in the room plus an outhouse in the back yard. The only source of heat coming up from the kitchen below did little to counteract the cold

wind and fog. The biggest problem, though, was the fleas. Eugene didn't seem to mind them too much, but according to Georges, he was being "eaten alive."

Since there was no restaurant in the hotel, the guests ate dinner with the Grisinghers. The nightly routine consisted of the table being cleaned off and Mr. Grisingher pulling out a deck of cards and insisting that the two men join the couple in a game. With no other place to go, and not wanting to hurt the man's feelings, the LeRoys joined in the game.

Each morning the brothers hired a horse and buggy and set out to inspect their newly acquired rancho lands, using the maps and notes given to them by Rudolph Steinbach, their uncle's former property manager. In making these inspections, the two became acquainted with Antonio and Peter Tognazzini, the Pezzonis, Perinonis, Silvas, Morgantis, Mattisons, Clarks, Saulsburys, and Johnstons. Georges developed a lasting friendship with both Clark and Saulsbury.

Having been told before his departure from France that he'd probably have to visit the ranchos, Eugene brought with him some of the work clothes that he'd worn on his farm in France, including heavy shoes and corduroy pants. Although the ranchers overlooked the man's shoes, the corduroy pants were too much for the dairy farmers to ignore. "Come here and meet the French boy in velvet pants!" Although Eugene didn't appreciate the chiding, he took it in good grace.

After a few weeks the brothers returned to San Francisco, both concerned about the lack of boundaries separating the properties. The property needed to be surveyed.

For the next fourteen years the LeRoy brothers

made periodic trips to Guadalupe to survey every inch of their property. In doing so, they endeared themselves to the town's ranchers and farmers.

Their discomfort in facing the perils of the willows, thorns and chaparral was exceeded only by the danger of quicksand. The areas near the Guadalupe Lake, Oso Flaco and the Coralitos Mesa were treacherous. Worse, though, was the Santa Maria River, especially that section from the town of Guadalupe to the ocean, which had deep pits of quicksand. As late at the 1920's Charlie Marretti lost a number of cattle there.

Both Eugene and Georges had some close calls, a few times losing their shoes and even some of their expensive surveying instruments.

In 1888, the brothers took the narrow gauge to Santa Maria, where Stephen Campodonico met them at the train stop.

As far as luxury was concerned, the trip by railroad wasn't much of an improvement over the schooner. The engine was a wood-burner and there were grades that it could hardly manage. The passengers would help by carrying loads of firewood (which had been stacked here and there along the tracks) to the engine in order to build up more steam, thereby enabling the train to climb the difficult grade. Sometimes the freight, mostly lumber, would get jostled and fall to the ground. Again the passengers would be called upon to lend a hand in reloading the car. Occasionally, when the train would jump the track, everyone on board was called upon to get out and help lift it back on the rails. With all these problems, the train was never on time.

When Georges, who had been so mercilessly attacked by fleas during his first trip, heard that the leaves of the eucalyptus tree would keep the insects away, he began bringing with him an extra suitcase filled with eucalyptus leaves. As soon as he'd arrive at the Grisingher Hotel, he'd start placing layers of the leaves under the mattress, under the bed, and wherever else he thought they might do some good. He claimed that the fleas never bothered him again.

Throughout the years, Eugene and Georges worked to save Theodore's empire. Eugene's hard, stubborn, and legally trained mind, plus the tenacity of the two brothers, resulted in their retaining the vast Rancho property. People with less determination and ability might not have been as successful.

After the brothers died, Eugene's two sons, Eugene Rene and Andre, inherited the property. Georges had never married and had no children.

When many of the townspeople left Guadalupe and moved to Santa Maria, the Portuguese and Swiss/Italian farmers stayed to run their farms and dairies in Guadalupe and Oso Flaco, with many of them leasing property from the LeRoys. Tony Olivera remembered his father leasing dairy property in Oso Flaco from the LeRoys in the 1930s for $20 an acre. When the property taxes were increased, the contract was changed to include the payment of such taxes.

The respect accorded Eugene Rene LeRoy knew no bounds. The man had a strong feeling for the land and took great pride in his family's careful stewardship. He had an equal respect for his tenants who shared his love for the land. When times were tough, he worked with them, thus enabling them to continue to farm the land despite their personal and economic problems.

Clarence Minetti, whose father-in-law began leasing property from the LeRoys in 1911, said that the name of LeRoy was the most respected name among the farmers in the valley. Jack Adam, Emilio Sutti, the Cossas, the Guggias and the Ferinis all knew the man well. Eugene Rene LeRoy passed away in 1985.

This venture began at the start of the Gold Rush when Victor Leroy pulled his ship into a port in Peru and saw the dock loaded with wildly excited people who couldn't wait to get to the gold mines. Because of that unexpected incident, and Victor's decision to seize the opportunity, plus Theodore's hardheaded business acumen, the LeRoy name has become engraved in the history of Guadalupe. ❧

The Dana Story

ARÍA JOSEFA PETRA DEL CARMEN CARRILLO, the eldest of eight children born to Don Carlos Antonio Carrillo and María Josefa (Castro) Carrillo, was only 12 years old when the brig *Waverly*, with Capt. William Goodwin Dana at the helm, first dropped anchor in Santa Barbara in 1824. The following year, the captain opened a store in Santa Barbara, but placed it in the charge of Capt. C. R. Smith while he continued to command his ship on its many voyages on the Pacific.

It is believed that Captain Dana and Josefa first met about this time, thus beginning a three-year courtship.

On March 22, 1828, Dana petitioned General José María de Echeandia for permission to marry Doña María Josefa Carrillo. Six weeks later the governor replied that since Dana's application for citizenship, forwarded to Mexico the previous January, hadn't been acted upon, further proceedings would have to be delayed, in accordance with the law.

However, the governor's office advised him that if nothing happened to the contrary, the question would definitely be settled in five months.

Dana was neither a Mexican citizen nor a Catholic, both prerequisites for marriage to a *señorita* (and ultimately, to obtain a land grant) during those days when California was a territory of Mexico.

The Carrillo family, holding much prestige throughout the state, ranked high among the wealthiest families in Santa Barbara at a time when a man was inclined to marry as much for wealth as for beauty. Not only were the Carrillos related to the prestigious De La Guerra family, but José Castro, Josefa's maternal uncle, was the military commander of California.

Capt. Dana converted to Catholicism in 1827. According to Myron Angel's *History of San Luis Obispo,* he became a Mexican citizen in February of 1828, but the certificate of naturalization, signed by José Figueroa, didn't actually come until February of 1835.

After becoming a Mexican citizen, he was appointed Captain of the Port at Santa Barbara. In 1836 he became *Alcalde* (mayor) of Santa Barbara.

On August 20, 1828, the 32-year-old Capt. Dana and the 16-year-old Josefa were married in Santa Barbara, where they continued to live until 1839. The couple's first daughter, María Josefa, was born on July 9, 1829. Of the 21 children born to the couple, seven girls and 14 boys, seven died in infancy, and Adelina Eliza, the twelfth child, died a few months after reaching her fifth birthday.

On April 6, 1837, Dana was awarded the 37,888-acre Mexican land grant, Rancho Nipomo, which stretched from near the shores of the Pacific Ocean on the west to the foot of the Santa Lucia Mountain to the east. It was there that he built his adobe on a hill that offered a panoramic view of the countryside "as far as the eye could see."

In the fall of 1839, Dana moved his family to the Rancho, where he became heavily engaged in stock raising, farming and manufacturing.

The family had many visitors at the adobe at a time when roads from rancho to rancho were nothing but trails and people traveled either by horseback or by carreta.

Although the generosity and hospitality of the captain's wife were reported to have been legendary, not much has been written about her, since most women at that time took a back seat to their men.

When the Captain died in 1858, the Nipomo Grant was left in trust to his widow, with the understanding that all profits and increases in the herds would go to her. After her death, the herds and land were to be equally divided among the children, except for the Pollards, who had already been well provided for.

María Josefa Dana Tefft was appointed Trustee, a position that she was to hold until she re-married. Her first husband, Henry A. Tefft, the first Assemblyman from San Luis Obispo County, had drowned in 1850. When she married Sam Pollard in 1854, four years before her father died, her brother William was appointed to succeed her. When William resigned because he was moving to San José, Charles was offered the job, but he declined the offer, as he was too busy with politics and business enterprises in San Luis Obispo. John

Francis accepted the Trusteeship, a position which he kept until 1882, when the Rancho was divided.

In 1882, while the widow Josefa was still alive, the family decided to divide the ranch. To accomplish the division, it was agreed to make fifteen different parcels, twelve to provide for each of the children, with the exception of the Pollards. However, since the Pollard children no longer owned any property—their mother had died in 1878—an equal section was made for them.

The fourteenth section of the divided land was for Josefa, and approximately 10,500 acres were set aside to adjust for any inequities in the other parcels.

According to Alonzo P. Dana, grandson of Captain and Mrs. Dana, a modern two-story house, entirely made of wood, was completed for the widow in 1880. Windows on all four sides gave her a view of the hills for miles around. María Josefa lived in her elegant home, surrounded by her many children and grandchildren, until she passed away on September 25, 1883. When the house fell from its foundation some years later, it was demolished.

Both Josefa and Captain Dana are buried in the Old Mission Cemetery on South Higuera Street in San Luis Obispo.

Isaac Fesler

 SAAC AND NANCY (BARNES) Fesler, donors of property that became one of Santa Maria's famous Four Corners, came to California by wagon train from Linn County, Missouri, in 1865, settling first in Sonoma County. The trip westward was long and arduous, with the older children walking most of the way. Sons Steven and Sterling walked ahead of the wagon train to serve as water scouts.

After arriving in California, the family made a series of moves before heading for the Santa Maria Valley. Mary Catherine, the couple's youngest child and the only daughter to survive childhood, was born in a covered wagon on March 21, 1867, in Solano.

In 1869, when Isaac heard about good farming in the southern California area, he packed up his family and headed for the Central Coast area. He came into the Santa Maria Valley by way of the Cuyamas to claim 160 acres of homestead land in the area then known as Grangeville. The property on which he farmed and built his house was located on what is now the 100 block of West Fesler Street.

Sadly, Emily, the couple's first daughter, as well as James and Silas, died in a flu epidemic shortly after arriving in Grangeville, later known as Central City. By 1882 the town's name had changed to Santa Maria.

On January 31, 1875, Fesler sold a piece of his property to L. M. Kaiser, who built a clothing store. The Kaiser Brothers store was later sold to Samuel Coblentz and Alfred Weilheimer, who served the town as Weilheimer and Coblentz until 1891, when L. M. Schwabacher purchased Weilheimer's interest. The two popular men operated Schwabacher and Coblentz until 1932, when they retired.

On October 4, 1885, Rev. McCann officiated at the marriage of eighteen-year-old Mary Catherine Fesler and 25-year-old James C. Martin at the Methodist Episcopal Church. Martin, who had come west from Missouri, first settled in Salinas, where he and a partner opened a store. As sometimes happens, the partner ran off with all of the money and stock. With limited finances, Martin came to Central City, arriving in the town on his twenty-first birthday in 1880. For a time he ran a newspaper/magazine store in the center of town.

James and Mary Catherine had three children. Lorena, their only daughter, was born in 1889 and attended schools in Santa Maria. She was still a small child when the family moved to Colorado, where Martin worked in his brother's silver mine. From Colorado, the family returned to Martin's roots in Missouri

The Martins returned to Santa Maria in about 1927, and James went to work for the county, taking care of the old Pioneer Park at Tepusquet. The couple lived in a little house in that remote area until about 1932, when boys from the local high school began to go out there to cause trouble and "make mischief." Afraid to be so far out of town, the Martins returned to Santa Maria. In 1932, four years before he died, Martin worked with a crew of men planting trees in Washington Grove, later to become Waller Park.

Isaac Fesler, who had married Nancy Barnes in 1841, passed away on July 24, 1891. Nancy, who was born February 12, 1822, in Tennessee, passed away in Santa Maria on August 22, 1895.

After Jim Martin passed away in 1936, Mary Catherine lived in a small apartment on Mill Street until her eyesight began to fail her and she couldn't be left alone. She moved from her apartment into the home of her grandson, Bill Briscoe, and his wife, Mabel. Her health steadily declined until she passed away in 1954 at the age of 87; she was buried next to her husband in the Santa Maria Cemetery.

James F. Goodwin

OMESTEADERS IN CENTRAL City were frustrated. Although most of them were experienced farmers, they couldn't get the sand to stop moving long enough for seedlings to take root. The gale-like winds needed to be contained, but how?

James F. Goodwin, who was born in 1855, was barely a year old when he left the territory of Nebraska with his family and started the long, weary trek across the overland route to California, headed for Lassen County. Ten years later, the family moved to Los Angeles, where young James lived for seven years before coming to the Santa Maria Valley.

When Goodwin arrived in the wind-swept dust bowl then known as Central City, he couldn't help but notice the unbroken monotony of the valley and the damage done to the crops by the untamed winds. It was then that the idea of planting trees took root in his mind. However, that was a project for the future. First he had to make a living.

Two years after Goodwin's arrival in town, he opened a small general store. He later took in William A. Haslam and William Adam, Jr. as partners.

During this time, while still mulling over the idea of planting trees to protect the crops from the cutting sand, he decided to go into the tree-growing business. Within two years he had planted more than 40,000 eucalyptus seedlings. In 1888, when the need for more trees became apparent, Goodwin joined with L. E. Blochman, William Laird Adam and Jeff Jones in hiring two men to plant both blue and red gum seeds in boxes for later transplanting throughout the valley.

With the townspeople having to go out to Guadalupe to pick up their mail, Goodwin was instrumental in getting a post office in the growing hamlet of Santa Maria; he became the town's first postmaster.

By 1890, Goodwin had sold his interest in the store to Haslam and had joined the Board of Directors of the newly formed Bank of Santa Maria, where Paul Tietzen served as manager. Goodwin also worked as a cashier at the bank.

Goodwin was known to wear many hats, and he became personally connected with the growth of his adopted city. When the Pinal Oil Company incorporated in 1901, Goodwin served with D. D. Bernard and Pat Moore as director. The company began drilling in September of 1902 and found oil the following November. The Pinal Oil and Dome Oil Companies merged in 1912 and finally sold out to the Union Oil Company in 1917.

The Santa Maria Realty Company, the predecessor of Santa Maria Gas and Power Company, was organized in March of 1906, with Goodwin and Tietzen serving as directors. Although gas pipes were put down from the Brookshire Oil Lease to Santa Maria, people were skeptical, feeling that the yield of gas was not substantial enough and would bring only a temporary source of power.

By April of 1917, natural gas was turned into the city's distributing system, and by the end of the month the firm was supplying 30 customers, with many of them living in fear that the gas would fail at any minute, leaving them all stuck with useless new appliances.

Goodwin served as president of the Gas Company from 1913 to 1928 when his son, Guy, took over. Guy served as president until the following year, when Bob Easton took over the helm.

Both Mr. and Mrs. Goodwin were interested in both public and private welfare movements of the community. Mrs. Goodwin, a founding member of the Minerva Club, persuaded her husband to donate the land located at the corner of Lincoln and Boone Streets, property which later became the home of the club.

In a speech later made at a Santa Maria Pioneer Association picnic, L. E. Blochman said, "Of all the persons of Santa Maria, none were so outstanding and prominent as the late James F. Goodwin. No other single person was so intimately connected throughout its history and development as that genial personality who, for fifty years, made his home in the Santa Maria Valley."

James F. Goodwin passed away in 1928 and is buried in the Santa Maria Cemetery.

The Adam Family

ILLIAM LAIRD ADAM, the eleventh of twelve children of William Thom and Isabella Laird Adam, was born in Lanarkshire, Scotland, in 1836. Isabella died when William was about 8 years old and his father married a much younger woman.

An adventure that was to change Adam's life forever began in September of 1850, when the family left Liverpool, England, headed for Salt Lake City, where the Mormons were in the process of building their city and temple.

In his hand-written memoirs, Adam described traveling by ship across the Atlantic Ocean to New Orleans, and then up the Mississippi River to Council Bluffs, Iowa, and then on to Salt Lake City with a Mormon wagon train. Adam left the Mormon settlement and finally arrived in San Bernardino in the fall of 1854 at the age of 18.

He eventually wound up in San Jose, California, where he met and married Elizabeth "Bessie" Conner, who had come to California from Frampton, Quebec, by way of the Isthmus of Panama. The Adam family eventually moved to Watsonville.

In 1869, two years after Benjamin Wiley had arrived in the vast wasteland known as the Santa Maria Valley and staked his claim of government land, the Adam family, driving a herd of cattle, was heading south.

By the time that Adam, his wife Bessie and their five children, William Conner, Mary, Isabelle, James and Charles Augustus, arrived in the valley, there were about 100 people living here,

with more planning to come. Alexander Adam, William's brother, also accompanied the family.

The Adam family settled on acreage near the river. On Thanksgiving Day Adam finished building a house for his family, had already dug a well, and by Christmas Day was producing his own water.

Shortly after the first of the year, Adam opened a store on the road to Guadalupe, taking everything that the farmers brought him in lieu of money, then shipping the goods from Port Harford to San Francisco. His store had a false front and the sides were of board-and-batten construction. He sold brown sugar from barrels, as well as lard, flour, green coffee beans and, occasionally, canned fruit.

Until the narrow gauge came through in 1882, all supplies were freighted in from Port Harford. In 1884 Adam sold the store to his son, William Conner and James F. Goodwin, who moved the business to the corner of Main and Broadway in Santa Maria.

By the time the youngest child was born in 1886, the Adam family had increased to twelve children, with Thomas Bernard, Anastasia, Margaret, Kenneth, Katherine, Carlyle Alexander and Anne Elizabeth having been born in the Santa Maria Valley.

Anastasia, Kenneth, Margaret and Thomas Bernard Adam were all baptized in Central City by Father John McNally on July 25, 1875. Three-year-old Margaret died in 1877 and Kenneth died in 1899.

In 1888 Adam financed the planting of gum

trees by James Goodwin and L. E. Blochman in an effort to stop the untamed winds.

By July of 1890, Adam and Goodwin were tapping water at Fugler's Point and bringing the water down as far as the William H. Rice ranch (located about 1½ miles east on the present East Stowell Road), thus introducing irrigation to the valley.

After selling his store, Adam engaged principally in stock-raising and farming on the more than 9,000 acres of land that he acquired in both Huasna and Santa Maria, the largest acreage being in Huasna.

The eldest of the Adam sons, William Conner Adam, born in 1861, was eight years old when the family moved into the valley from Watsonville. The settlers found the land fertile and immediately responsive to cultivation. Wheat, which matured early, was the principal crop. A major problem throughout the valley was the lack of water and, of course, the wind.

Lumber came into the valley on ships that periodically visited Cave Landing. Since there was no landing chute, lumber was merely dumped overboard and allowed to float to shore, with the hopes that the waves wouldn't pound it to pieces before it reached the beach.

The lumber, not being graded, came in all lengths and widths. Thus, the finished product left much to be desired.

William Conner Adam married Ida Kelly in January of 1888 in a ceremony performed in Guadalupe by the Reverend Michael Lynch.

James E. Adam, born in Watsonville in 1866, attended local public schools. After graduating from Santa Clara College, he returned to the valley, where he worked with his father on the ranch property.

In April of 1892, James married Mary A. Donovan, daughter of Patrick Donovan, in a ceremony performed in Los Berros by the Reverend Michael Lynch. The couple had six children.

Charles Augustus married Jane Porter in 1896 at St. Patrick's Church in Arroyo Grande; in 1898 Isabelle "Belle" married Patrick Henry Sheehy in Santa Maria; in 1899 Anastasia "Nessie" Adam married Isaac Porter in Santa Maria; and in 1909 Annie Elizabeth married Leo Preisker in San Luis Obispo.

Katherine Adam married Joe Rembusch; Carlyle "Carl" married May Lafferty, and Thomas Bernard married Grace Thornburgh, daughter of Jesse Thornburgh. Mary "Lade" Adam never married.

After William Laird Adam arrived in the Santa Maria Valley in 1869, there was never a time when he wasn't involved in the betterment of his chosen community. Deeply interested in making education available to everyone, he was one of the advocates of the Agricola School, which was built in 1875; the East Main Street School, built in 1881; and the high school, built in 1891.

Until his death in 1903 he was a consistent worker for the welfare of the valley and its people. Elizabeth Conner Adam had died in 1898. Both are buried in the Santa Maria Cemetery. 🙚

The Wineman Family

ATHERINE BINGOLD, born in Germany in 1848, arrived in New York in the mid-1860s and, like many female im-migrants of the time, she worked as a domestic.

She met Edward Wineman (whose family name of Wein-mann had been Americanized at Ellis Island) at one of the little neighborhood German parties, and the two were later married. Knowing that being proficient in the English language was a necessity in their adopted coun-try, the Winemans attended English classes at a night school in their area.

In the late 1860s the Wine-mans came to Los Baños, where they used government land to graze sheep.

In 1879, Edward, Catherine, and their three children led a herd of sheep to San Luis Obispo County, where they rented the southern part of the Rancho Nipomo, located along-side the Santa Maria River. Two years later they bought part of the property.

In addition to raising sheep and cattle, the Winemans be-gan to purchase bankrupt property, and became one of the most prosperous families in the valley.

The colonial house that they built to house their nine chil-dren, six boys and three girls, became the showplace of the area. Catherine had personally selected the furniture during a trip to San Francisco, where she also bought gold watches for each of her children.

When dry years hit the Central Coast, Edward Wine-man took his cattle north to Solano County, where he felt that water would be more plen-tiful. However, after a few years of stifling hot summers and unbearably cold winters, he was happy to return to his ranch in Nipomo.

When wool prices fell in the 1890s, the Winemans built a warehouse to store the wool until the economy improved. When the price of wool went up, they were able to sell it at a considerable profit.

After her children had grown up, Catherine became active in the Republican Party.

When William McKinley ran for the presidency and promised

Edward and Catherine Wineman

28

to levy an import tax on wool, thus increasing domestic wool prices, Catherine did some hard campaigning for him, and announced that if the man were elected, she'd throw a blowout celebration with a free supper and dance for everyone.

True to her word, when McKinley won the election, the Winemans threw the promised barbecue on Friday, the 13th of November, 1896, at Knott's Hall. With George May and J. A. Donovan serving as floor managers, the merrymakers danced until dawn to the music of Nipomo's String Band. When the clock struck twelve, the banquet began. Food was spread out on the tables, covering them from end to end.

Edward and Catherine Wineman helped spearhead the building of St. Joseph's Catholic Church in Nipomo from 1898 to 1903.

"All went as merry as the marriage bell," with some remarking that they wished that the Republicans would win every election. The big splash was the talk of the area for many years afterwards.

Although McKinley was elected for two terms, he was assassinated on September 6, 1906, shortly after a visit to this area. After his death, Theodore Roosevelt, McKinley's vice-president, was sworn in as president.

During those early years, with no Catholic church in Nipomo, the town's Catholics rode by horse and buggy to attend Mass in either Arroyo Grande or Guadalupe. Nipomo needed a Catholic church of its own. Catherine rose to the task by working as an untiring chairperson in soliciting donations from the local residents.

From 1898 to 1903 she supervised the construction of the church at the corner of Tefft Street and Thompson Avenue, with her sons carting rocks and stones for the foundation from the Wineman Ranch.

After the church was finally built and Catherine was given the honor of naming it, she chose to name it after St. Joseph, the patron saint of the working man.

The stained-glass windows, engraved with the names of Machado, Serpa, Lucas, Madruga, Rose, Dana, Sheehy, Brown and Donovan, stood in silent testimony to the people who gave their time and money in making the Nipomo's first Catholic church a reality. The Winemans donated the window dedicated to St. Joseph.

As the years progressed and Nipomo became more populated, the parish outgrew the little church. A larger church was built, and the stained-glass windows from the original church of St. Joseph were installed in the new building. The first services were held on March 29, 1968, at the new church on Thompson Avenue.

The little church on the corner of Tefft Street and Thompson Road was sold and served as a wedding chapel.

Both Edward Wineman, who passed away in 1921, and Catherine, who died nine years later, are buried in the Old Mission Cemetery in San Luis Obispo. ☙

ILLUSTRATION BY DANIEL MARTIN

The Hart House Hotel

HEN JUSTICE OF THE PEACE Madison Thornburgh performed the marriage ceremony of 34-year-old Harriet Sharp and Reuben Hart on December 31, 1878, Hart was one of the most influential men in the city, with his name figuring into almost every industry in Central City.

Ten years later, when the couple opened the Hart House on the southeast corner of East Main Street and Broadway with a spectacular dinner and ball, their new hotel was one of the most elegant show places in California.

Built by the pioneer Doane Building Company, this magnificent hotel boasted a spacious lobby, office, reading room, bar, barbershop, a stationery store on the first floor, and a huge dining room.

In addition to the single rooms and suites on the second floor, the hotel also featured a parlor and a front veranda. Beautiful chandeliers hung in the suites, with fireplaces in every room. With lavishly decorated high-headboard beds, lace curtains hanging in every window, with some rooms even having marble-topped dressers and commodes, the Hart House was the accomplishment of the century.

The interior was lavishly furnished and decorated in the Victorian style of the 1890s, with the furniture coming all the way from San Francisco. In spite of the fact that the hotel was the epitome of luxury, the building had no central heating system and the rooms had no water, electricity nor telephones.

In addition to the stables that Hart kept for the horse and buggy trade, the Hart House main-

tained a horse-drawn transportation system, with a seating capacity of sixteen, to carry guests between the hotel and the railroad station in Guadalupe. Hart also provided a single horse and buggy for his family.

Samuel Sharp, father of Harriet Sharp Hart, who also lived at the Hart House, became a fixture of the hotel as he spent his days sitting in a huge rocking chair, chatting with the guests as they came in. Later, when he learned that the hotel was about to be leased and the family would be moving out, he went into depression and his health began to decline. He passed away in December of 1893, just a few months before the family moved out of the hotel.

Reuben and Harriet Hart owned, managed and lived in the Hart House, together with their daughter Harriet, for about six years before leasing it out. When they finally sold out to Charles Bradley, the name was changed to "The Bradley House."

Shortly after the change of ownership took place, the guests were able to ride in one of those new-fangled autos, controlled by a single lever steering gear, and sporting a fringed top and open-air sides.

The glamour of the Gay '90s eventually disappeared and the hotel slowly went into disrepair. It was finally abandoned in 1968, the year before it burned to the ground.

After the Harts sold their hotel they moved into a house on East Church Street. Later, after the turn of the century, they moved into their large home at 606 South Broadway, where the water works was located.

Harriet Sharp Hart died of stomach cancer in 1896, when young Hattie was in her early teens. Reuben and Hattie, who later married George Scott, continued living in the house on South Broadway until he passed away in 1923. The house was sold to the city and later became the site of the Santa Maria Plunge.

Santa Maria High School

HE SANTA MARIA HIGH School District, among the oldest high school districts in the state, has a history of producing some of the nation's top leaders, scholars and athletes.

While only four students graduated from the school in 1894 (in Lucas Hall, as the school was still under construction), interested townspeople and dedicated educators Ida Twitchell Blochman and George C. Russell worked hard to attain State University accreditation. This was achieved in 1902, when the school had only four teachers on its staff.

Through the years, more buildings and general improvements were made. In 1921 the original building was torn down, and the new building was completed two years later.

In 1963, in order to comply with earthquake specifications, the bell tower was torn down, the auditorium and theater facilities were reduced in size, and the school's second story was condemned and closed for educational purposes. After the building had met governmental requirements, the auditorium was dedicated to Ethel Pope, a much-loved teacher who had taught at the school for many years.

Until World War II ended and the city's population exploded, the school's location was far from the center of town. Students stuck close to the campus because there was no place else to go. Steve, the candy and ice cream man, made daily trips to the school, parking his made-over Model T at Morrison Avenue and Lincoln Street.

Although the vehicle looked like a cracker box, according to Bill Bright, Steve sold the "best peanut brittle in the world, and for only 5 cents."

As the years passed, each class produced students who went on to distinguish themselves, on both local and national levels.

George Hobbs, Class of 1937, served as Mayor of Santa Maria for many years; Richard Chenoweth, Class of 1959, became Director and Curator of the Santa Maria Historical Museum. Shirley Juarez Boydstun, Class of 1945, went into nursing, earning a degree as Stanford. Bill Bright, who once ran a filling station on the site of the present Vandenberg Inn and later went into the oil business, graduated with the class of 1935. Marilyn Hoback Cronk, Class of 1954, became Director of the Elverhoj Museum of History and Arts in Solvang. George Aratani, Class of 1935, was a member of the high school team that won the 1932 CIF championship in San Diego. Mr. Aratani later became a member of the United States Japanese Intelligence Service. When World War II ended, he began building All Star Trading, the parent company of Mikasa. Russ Manning, class of 1946, was a famed illustrator of the Tarzan comic strips. George Curtis Tunnell, prominent business leader, one-time mayor of Santa Maria and member of the Santa Barbara Board of Supervisors, graduated in June of 1927. Morris Stephan, who served as Judge of the Superior Court of Santa Barbara, graduated with the Class of 1923.

On a national level, Owen Siler, Class of 1938 (whose father was an accounting teacher at the high school), became Commandant of the United

States Coast Guard. Gordon Hartley, Class of 1935, was distinguished as being captain of the aircraft carrier that retrieved the first space capsule. Jim May, Class of 1939, retired in 1977 after serving thirty-one years with the U. S. State Department Diplomatic and Consular Corps.

The high school has produced many world class swimmers. John Paulsen, Class of 1933, swam in the Olympics as part of the United States Swimming team in 1932; Eugene Lenz, Class of 1955, competed in the Olympic Games in Italy in 1964.

Joe Gularte Soares, Class of 1933, was a trainer with the New York Yankees for 26 years, while Les Webber, Class of 1935, pitched in major league baseball for five years. John Rudometkin, Class of 1958, played with both the New York Knickerbockers and the San Francisco Warriors. Bryn Smith, Class of 1973, went on to pitch for the Montreal Expos. Bradley Dandridge, Class of 1989, played for one of the Dodgers' farm teams.

After World War II ended, Cappy Harada, Class of 1940, received an assignment from General Douglas MacArthur to revive professional and college sports in occupied Japan, thus becoming commissioner of baseball in Japan. He later became a special advisor to the Yomiuri Giants professional team, the last Japanese team to conduct spring training in the United States.

Many other graduates distinguished themselves in their own fields of endeavor. Names of Santa Maria High School graduates can be found in many business and professional rosters through-

The bell tower at Santa Maria High School's Ethel Pope Auditorium was a Santa Maria landmark until it was torn down in 1963 as an earthquake hazard.

out the country.

The loving respect that the former graduates have for the school is manifested when the school holds its annual alumni banquet, which is always held the night before the annual Pioneer Picnic. It's a time when they all either come home to attend the dinner, or send their best wishes from wherever life has taken them.

Winston Wickenden

T O KNOW THE HISTORY of Winston Wickenden is to know the history of Santa Barbara County. The man was able to count among his ancestors the Foxens, the Cotas and the Osunas. Frederick and Ramona (Foxen) Wickenden were his paternal grandparents, while Fred and Louisa Kriegel of Los Alamos were his maternal grandparents. The Goodchild, Arata, Lugo, de la Guerra, Carteri and Olivera families were all early Mexican Rancho era names that figured prominently into the Foxen/Wickenden history.

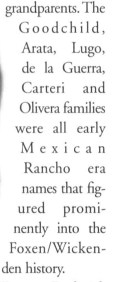

Winston Frederick Wickenden (so named at Frederick Wickenden's request to honor Winston Churchill) was born May 30, 1905, in Los Alamos to John Richard and Flora M. (Kriegel) Wickenden. He was baptized at the San Ramón Chapel, a church that his grandparents, Frederick and Ramona (Foxen) Wickenden, had built in 1875. His cousin, Abdon Ontiveros, grandson of Juan Pacífico Ontiveros, served as his godfather.

Winston received his early education in Los Alamos. When he was about eight years of age, his family moved to a house that his father had built on South Broadway. He attended both the West Fesler School and the East Main Street School (located where Wells Fargo was later built), and graduated from Santa Maria High School with the class of 1923½.

Mr. Wickenden showed his business acumen at an early age when he was appointed manager of the *Review* during his senior year at the high school. He instituted a prepayment system for the purchase of the book whereby students were required to make a deposit of $1.00 each towards the purchase of the annual, which could be redeemed when the book was actually issued. This system produced the first time in the school's history that the annual publication did not wind up in the red, bringing much relief to the members of the Board of Trustees, who had formerly used their own money to cover any shortages.

Wickenden was enrolled at the University of California at Berkeley and was scheduled to begin classes in the fall of the year, but since he graduated from high school at such an odd time of the year, he had six months with noth-

The San Ramón Chapel was built by Frederick and Ramona Foxen Wickenden at the mouth of Foxen Canyon in 1875.

ing to do. After persuading Frank McCoy, then serving as president of the Golf Club, to permit him to become a Junior member of the club in order to satisfy the university's physical education requirements, Winston played golf until he entered Berkeley the following August.

After graduating from Berkeley, Winston went to work for Libby McNeil in the Stockton area, and remained with the company until 1944, when his father was ready to retire and asked him to come home to run the ranch.

Always civic minded, Mr. Wickenden served on the first Santa Maria Airport Board of Directors and as a director of the Santa Maria Savings & Loan Association on West Cypress Street. While

serving as president of the Rotary Club, he helped set up Rotary clubs in Mexico. For his efforts he was made a Lifetime Member of the Rotary organization. Throughout his life he participated in just about every organized effort for the betterment of the Santa Maria Valley.

Mr. Wickenden always had a story to tell, and was proud of his ancestors, particularly Frederick and Ramona Wickenden, who were responsible for the building of San Ramón Chapel.

During the early days of the valley, the Santa Inés Mission was the only church in the area. Because of the long distance to travel, settlers found it difficult to attend mass. In order to serve Catholics in the area, priests from the Mission would walk from the Mission to the outlying communities to administer the Sacraments, but not on a regular basis.

In 1875, the year after Benjamin Foxen died, his son-in-law, Frederick Wickenden, drove 5,000 sheep up to Redwood City, where he sold them for $1 each. With his profits he not only purchased redwood lumber with which to add on to his adobe, but also enough lumber to build a chapel on his property so that the Catholics in Sisquoc would have a place of worship close to home.

With the help of Fred and Thomas Foxen and Chris Clausen, a carpenter from Los Alamos, the little church was built using the lumber from Redwood City. The following year the coffin containing the remains of Benjamin Foxen was taken from the pasture in back of his adobe and reinterred in the chapel cemetery at the insistence of his daughter, Ramona.

In 1879 the chapel was both completed and dedicated as the San Ramón Chapel. Services were held once a month, with Reverend Michael Lynch serving the Mission until 1886, when St. Patrick's Church in Arroyo Grande was built and he became pastor of the new church.

Through the ensuing years the spiritual needs of the Sisquoc community were met by various priests from the Santa Inés Mission. In 1908 it was turned over to the newly established St. Mary's of the Assumption church in Santa Maria.

However, the San Ramón Chapel fell into serious disrepair and was closed from 1908 to 1933 except for occasional funerals and baptisms. In 1936, a group of concerned people, led by Robert E. Easton, replaced the roof and painted the building. In 1958, Winston Wickenden initiated a major restoration project in which the wood post footings were replaced with a concrete block foundation.

In July of 1966, the Foxen Memorial Chapel became the first historical landmark in Santa Barbara County, with the dedication taking place on the following April 30th. In August of 1975, the San Ramón Chapel was designated as a California State Historical Landmark. Mass is currently being celebrated every Sunday by priests from the St. Louis de Montfort Church in Orcutt.

Mr. Wickenden was a highly respected man whose reputation as a great historian was well earned. When he passed away in September of 2000 at Marian Medical Center, the Santa Maria Valley lost a true friend.

In 1974, the San Ramón Chapel was used as the setting for an episode of CBS-TV's The Manhunter.

Irving Nolan McGuire

RVING NOLAN McGUIRE, son of James and Sarah McGuire, was born in Jackson County, Missouri, in 1832. Six years later the family moved to Buchanan County and stayed there eleven years before driving a team of oxen across the plains, headed for California.

The McGuires settled in Vacaville, where they built the first house in the community. Young Irving began raising cattle and horses, continuing in this venture until 1853, when he moved to Sonoma County. After buying 480 acres of land, he continued raising stock for another 20 years. In 1854 he married Sarah Condit of Sacramento.

McGuire moved again in 1873, this time to Oso Flaco, where he raised sheep and also served as Justice of the Peace. During the mid-seventies, when a diphtheria epidemic swept the area, the McGuires lost four of their ten children. When the severe drought of 1877 brought heavy losses to the early pioneer, he left the sheep-raising business and moved to San Luis Obispo, where he opened a mercantile store, a business that he ran until coming to Santa Maria in 1883 to open a drug store. He also served on the Board of Supervisors of San Luis Obispo County.

In May of 1887, McGuire bought out Stephen Clevenger's interest in the *Santa Maria Times* and became a partner with George Jenkins, the father-in-law of his daughter, Alice. McGuire remained active in the newspaper business until 1897, when he sold his interest in the newspaper to C. A. Seay of Carpinteria.

McGuire served as Master of the Guadalupe Masonic Lodge #237 in 1876, an organization that he had joined in September of 1874. The Guadalupe Masons, the oldest Masonic Order in the area, had organized the previous July. In November of 1876, John Mills Brown, Grand Master of Masons in the State of California, appointed Mr. McGuire Inspector for the Twenty-Eighth Masonic District.

In 1888, the year after Sarah died, McGuire married May Horseley. After the second Mrs. McGuire passed away in 1890, he moved in with his daughter, Alice Jenkins, and her husband. He passed away in June of 1910.

The six children of Irving Nolan McGuire and his wife, Sarah, included Oscar, William, Alice, Nellie, Sarah and Mortimer. Mortimer McGuire married Lulu Humbert and the couple had two children, Neal and Edna. Edna married Albert Roemer, and the couple had one child, Glenn. Glenn, who married Inez Ferini in 1936, had two sons, Vard and Robert.

Telephone Service in Santa Maria

N 1860, SIXTEEN YEARS after Samuel Morse first tapped out a simple message on his new invention, the telegraph, the Pacific & Atlantic Telegraph Company began to build a telegraph line down the coast. Beginning in San Francisco, the workmen began tacking wire to various trees on its way south, finally reaching Los Angeles on October 8 of that same year. The $2.50 charge for a ten-word message between San Francisco and Los Angeles was a hefty sum, considering that it was roughly equal to three days' pay for the average worker.

Sunset Telephone introduced the first telephone service to Santa Maria in 1891, generally following the old telegraph lines. Although the company functioned fairly well, lightning and roaming cattle often caused disruptions of service. The company built the first long-distance line between San Francisco and Los Angeles, completing the project in 1894.

Grace and Florence Clark, the first telephone operators in Santa Maria, operated a switchboard installed in a corner of their father's stationery store in the old Hart Hotel. The board, not more than two feet square, with holes for the plugs about an inch apart, only serviced about 20 businesses. At the sound of the buzzer, the girls would race to the switchboard (then called "centrals") and make the proper connection. The switchboard was only in operation during the daytime hours.

As the telephone grew in popularity, switch-

boards were installed in private homes. Carlotta "Lottie" (Campodonico) Acquistapace operated a "central" from her home in Guadalupe on what is now 9th Street.

According to Winston Wickenden, people in the Sisquoc area were required to install their own poles before the telephone company would agree to install its lines.

Sunset Telephone found competition in 1902, when a group of Los Angeles investors began laying the groundwork for a statewide network of independent telephone companies to compete with the Bell companies in nearly every city and town of substance. In 1906, three years after Home Telephone and Telegraph began operating in the Santa Barbara area, the company received a second franchise to operate in the north county area. Home Telephone and Telegraph Company of Santa Barbara County, with headquarters in Santa Maria, was incorporated on September 11, 1906, with Bob Easton at its helm.

When Pacific Telephone refused to permit Home Telephone to use its long-distance lines, Home responded by creating an independent company known as "The United States Long Distance Telephone Company." In spite of its grandiose name and the fact that it served most southern California cities, the new company had lines that only stretched as far north as Santa Maria. Therefore, the new company could neither make connections further north than Santa Maria, nor in any other state.

The problems of having two separate telephone companies were frustrating, as a customer of one company couldn't make contact with a person subscribing to a different company. In order to reach all of their customers, merchants were forced to subscribe to both companies.

Sunset was absorbed by its parent company, Pacific Telephone, in 1907.

In January of 1909, with Edna Teffin serving as chief operator, Pacific Telephone had 431 customers, while Home was a near tie, with 430 customers.

A "Farmer Line," so named because the line was owned and operated by its users, began a service between Santa Maria and Garey. However, not much information is available about the farmer service.

In April of 1916, when the two rival companies merged under the name of Santa Barbara Telephone Company, the entire county of Santa Barbara was serviced by just one company.

On December 31, 1939, with some 2400 lines in service, the Associated Telephone Company acquired the Santa Barbara Telephone Company and appointed Bob Easton as its Vice-President and Director.

Easton, a transplanted Bay area man, had his fingers in almost every business venture in the Santa Maria Valley. Holding a degree in engineering, he surveyed and fenced the Sisquoc Ranch and remained as its superintendent for 50 years. Living up to his reputation as being a man of uncanny ability to get things done, he became

Santa Maria switchboard operators posed for this group portrait during World War II.

active in many areas, all of which resulted in some benefit to the Santa Maria valley.

Bob Easton wore many hats. In addition to managing the Sisquoc Ranch, he was active in the development of the oil fields of Orcutt for the Pinal Dome Oil Company. He was active in the Santa Maria Realty Company in developing Santa Maria residential and farm lands and was an official of the First National Bank of Santa Maria. In 1909, he helped form the Santa Maria Gas Company, managed the Sisquoc Investment Company, and later, the telephone company.

With progress, the role of the rural telephones, those little boxes screwed into the wall with a crank on the side and a mouthpiece to talk into, as well as its central switchboards, were destined to disappear altogether. The year 1950 saw the end of manually operated switchboards in Santa Maria, when the telephone company converted to dial telephones. Some say, however, that operator assisted calls continued in Santa Maria until 1957.

In January of 1953, Associated Telephone Company became General Telephone Company.

Switchboards were located in various spots in Santa Maria, finally consolidating in the telephone company building that was built on the corner of Church and Lincoln Streets. When Santa Maria's west side was redeveloped in the mid-1980s, the building's neighbors were demolished. Today the telephone building borders the West Side Mall. ✥

The Coblentz Family

AMUEL COBLENTZ came to Santa Maria in 1884, when he and Alfred Weilheimer purchased the Kaiser Brothers store on the north side of West Main Street, next to the Bank of Santa Maria. Seven years later, in 1891, L. M. Schwabacher of San Francisco bought out Weilheimer's interest in the store, and two men operated as Coblentz and Schwabacher until they finally retired and closed the business in 1932.

Although the two partners had different political views, they remained staunch friends and were very much alike in their attitudes toward their customers, in whom they had an almost fatherly interest.

When the Coblentz family arrived in the town, sons Lambert ("Bert") and Edmond ("Edmo"), both born in the San Francisco area, were toddlers. Zach was born in 1893.

Santa Maria was a small town and only had a few churches. Since the Coblentz family was of the Jewish faith and the town had no synagogue at that time, Jewish services were held in the Methodist Church.

All three of the Coblentz boys received their early education in Santa Maria and graduated from Santa Maria Union High School.

After graduating from high school in 1897, Bert entered the University of California, but only stayed one year before transferring to the Cooper Medical College, where he graduated with the class of 1904. After serving as an intern with the Franklin Hospital in San Francisco, Dr. Lambert

Coblentz returned to Santa Maria, where he set up his practice with Dr. William T. Lucas in a building on the corner of Chapel and Vine streets.

During those early days, "Dr. Bert," as he came to be known, made his professional calls on horseback before graduating to a carriage and later to an automobile.

Dr. Bert joined the U. S. Army Medical Corps during World War I as a commissioned lieutenant and served two months as operating surgeon at the Presidio of Monterey before being promoted to Captain and assigned duty at Ft. Scott in San Francisco. He was later made operating surgeon at Ft. Worsen, Washington, where he stayed until the war was over. He rose to the rank of Major and was honorably discharged in December of 1918.

Although he returned to Santa Maria to resume his practice, he only stayed two years before going to New York City to take a special course in surgery. He pursued further studies both in Europe and at the prestigious Mayo Brothers Clinic in Rochester, Minnesota, before returning to Santa Maria.

Dr. Bert served as company doctor at the sugar factory in Betteravia, where each worker had $1 taken from his pay envelope per pay period to pay for his medical insurance.

When Dr. Lucas died in 1931, Dr. Bert took over his practice. With Dr. Bert specializing in surgical cases and his brother Dr. Zach being a general practitioner, the two built up a successful medical practice in Santa Maria.

In 1928 Dr. Bert moved to San Francisco, where he served on the staff at St. Luke's Hospital.

Apart from his medical practice, Dr. Bert was an avid hunter and fisherman. In January of 1949, he was out duck hunting when he found himself in muddy waters deeper than he had expected. His efforts to get out of the muck and mire triggered a heart attack, and the next day Dr. Lambert Coblentz passed away at St. Luke's Hospital. Funeral services were held in San Francisco.

Zach, who had begun practicing medicine in Santa Maria in 1931, moved in the middle 1930s to San Francisco, where he served as Chief of Obstetrics at Mount Zion Hospital.

Edmo's big break came in June of 1900, the year that he graduated from high school, when he entered a contest sponsored by William Randolph Hearst's *San Francisco Examiner.* Of the approximately 15,000 boys from throughout the state who took an examination about government and history, he was one of the 15 winners. His prize was a trip to the national Republican political convention in Philadelphia, where he witnessed the nomination of William McKinley and Theodore Roosevelt for the next presidential election.

Although Coblentz entered the University of California, he only stayed there a short time before being offered a job as a cub reporter for the *San Francisco Examiner,* thus beginning a career that was destined to bring him considerable fame within the Hearst Publications.

Twenty-five years after joining the *Examiner* he became the newspaper's publisher, and later spent 14 years as publisher of the *New York American* as well as supervising editor of all the Hearst papers. He returned to San Francisco to take over as publisher of the *San Francisco Call Bulletin,* his last full-time position before becoming editorial consultant of the entire Hearst newspapers.

Altogether, he spent over a half-century with the Hearst family of newspapers.

In May of 1941, during a speech at the Santa Maria Pioneer Association annual picnic,

Coblentz honored the memories of the early pioneers by dedicating his words to the men and women of yesteryear. He spoke of Mr. Long, the village blacksmith; Mr. McNeil, the miller; the Boyd brothers, "both farmers and outstanding men"; Mr. Fleisher; Mr. Goodwin and Dr. Lucas, "a country doctor who symbolized fellow service, if ever a man did"; the Jones family, and, of course, "Mr. Schwabacher and my own gentle father."

"The pioneers of Santa Maria built a community of self-reliant and sturdy citizens who left us a heritage of which we can all be proud. They set a standard of real human values that we can all adopt."

Coblentz recalled taking a chartered bus from Lierly's or Blosser's stables and spending almost a whole day in going to Pismo. A trip to San Francisco meant an overnight stopover in San Luis Obispo and a stage ride to pick up the train at Santa Margarita. To go to Los Angeles, one had to take the narrow gauge to Los Olivos, spend the night at Mattei's Tavern, and then ride the stage over the San Marcos Pass to Santa Barbara.

It was a time when,

if a kid didn't walk to school, he rode his bicycle or cart, or maybe went by horseback. The same child studied in the evening beneath the glow of a kerosene lamp, and went to bed by candlelight.

"The women of this community laid the foundation for a bigger, better and perhaps even a brighter future. The pioneer life was concentrated in a small place and among a few people, lending it qualities of companionship, understanding and satisfaction that were rich compensations.

"In the horse-and-buggy days the pioneer family, limited as it was to the home community, had a spiritual richness which had no better source, and probably no other source, than the company of friends and loved ones.

"We should not forget that while there were satisfactions and compensations in the pioneer life, there were also difficulties, privations and sacrifices. All our present facilities, the pleasant and comfortable living have the hardships and bitter tasks and unselfish services of our pioneer parents as their solid foundation. Their tears, sweat and toil made this country what it is."

Edmond D. Coblentz died of a heart attack on April 16, 1959, at the age of 76, at the Sonoma Valley Hospital.

The Newlove House

OHN NEWLOVE, BORN IN Lincolnshire County, England, on May 23, 1832, was 14 years of age when he left the old country to seek his fortune in the Toronto, Canada area.

After marrying Maria Benyon of Ontario, Canada, in December of 1860, the self-educated Newlove did some farming on rented land before trying his luck in the Golden State.

In 1864, he brought his family to California by way of the Isthmus of Panama. After spending some time in San Joaquin County and Santa Rita, he arrived in San Luis Obispo in 1873, where he began to raise stock.

A combination of luck and hard work brought Newlove a measure of success. In 1881 he moved his family to the Santa Maria Valley, where he bought more than 3,000 acres of land in the Mt. Solomon area and worked diligently to make the land one of the most valuable pieces of property in the area.

Having suffered through the cold fogs of his native England and the rigors of the harsh Canadian winters, Newlove dearly loved California, where the coastal country climate had no rival. Although his hard work and keen insight enabled him to accumulate large land tracts and extensive stock interests, he never lost interest in education and constantly worked for better schools.

After Newlove passed away in 1889, Maria continued to maintain the ranch home out in the Mt. Solomon area. When sheepherders in the area began knocking at the widow's door with offers to purchase her 3,000 acres, supposedly in order to raise sheep, she became suspicious. Why the sudden interest in her property?

When Western Oil Company put down a standard rig next to her property and found oil, Maria realized that she had oil on her land and was about to become a very rich woman.

Since this liquid gold seemed to be everywhere, the peaceful land where sheepherders once roamed the hills was thrown into a frenzy of excitement, and the people went wild with speculation.

When Pinal Oil Company, one of the many new companies being formed, was organized by James F. Goodwin, Paul Tietzen and other prominent men from Santa Maria, the group proceeded to purchase large tracts of oil property throughout the area. However, the rich Union Oil Company took the lead.

Not everyone became rich, though. Many local people lost fortunes when they invested heavily in smaller companies that failed to produce. It's been said that many a Santa Maria house was papered with worthless stock certificates. The promoters, though, were raking in a fortune.

Maria Newlove was one of the lucky ones. In 1904, when she sold her property outright to the Union Oil Company for 1.5 million dollars, she became one of the richest women in the valley. With her newfound riches, Maria was in a position to do pretty much as she pleased. She took her surviving eight children, accompanied by her seamstress and doctor, on a trip to Canada.

When Maria decided to build a grand house on her south Lincoln Street property, she contracted with the architectural firm of Wolfe and McKenzie of San Jose to design the high-style 17-room Colonial Revival house between South Broadway and Lincoln streets. In November of 1906, she signed a contract with the Doane Building Company of Santa Maria to build one of the most elegant houses in Santa Maria.

Right from the beginning, Maria, although demanding the beauty, elegance and charm befitting her new wealth, insisted that her mansion be part of a working farm. The upstairs rooms were to be used for the hired help, who, although using the traditional outside staircase to go to and from work, used the main staircase to join the family for meals.

Maria's 20-page list of specifications for the 17-room house went into great detail to insure that no short cuts would be taken and that quality would prevail.

As construction proceeded, electric bells and buzzers were placed strategically throughout the house. A speaking tube with a china mouthpiece was used in the upstairs hall to call down to the kitchen, and the elegant front door, decorated with carved rosettes around a large oval window, had a built-in buzzer.

The house had incandescent electric wiring and indoor plumbing throughout the house, and all interior work had three coats of paint. In addition, all of the oak floors were finished with one coat of shellac plus two coats of varnish.

The house, visible from South Broadway, was originally painted grayish-green, but was later repainted gray with white trim. Mrs. Newlove wasn't completely satisfied with either of those color schemes, so she finally had the clapboards painted white.

With furniture coming all the way from San Francisco, lace curtains on all of the windows, an extensive library, and beautiful wallpaper costing $2,000, Maria's house, the epitome of style and grace, became the showplace of the area.

Like many homes of its period, the Newlove house had a tall tank house and a granary nearby. In spite of its elegance, though, according to the family, "the plumbing never worked well."

The Newlove House, 1908

When Maria Newlove passed away in Pacific Grove in 1913, her son Ernest and his wife Myrtle inherited the house. The ghost of their son, Herman, who had been killed after being thrown from his horse, was said to have haunted the manor for many years. His ghostly figure, sometimes wearing a fancy collar and large bow about his neck while other times wearing spectacles, a stiff collar and a dark suit, often appeared at different times and places throughout the house. His figure was always timid and gentle, but never frightening.

As time passed and ownership changed, the old manor was used as a rental and the outside condition deteriorated.

However, in spite of the condition of the exterior of the house, the interior remained in good shape. In the early 1980s, when Dr. Ikola made plans to create a historical park, he purchased the Newlove House and had it moved to property that he'd purchased on the east side of highway 101 at Santa Maria Way. Plans for this historical park included not only the Newlove House, but also Dr. Ormond Paulding's house, which had been moved to make way for the Westside Mall, and the Pleasant Valley School, the first school built in the valley.

Dr. Ikola's plans for a historical park never materialized, as it became increasingly difficult for him to satisfy the requirements of the county officials. The Newlove House was finally sold to the Firestone family, who moved it out to its winery on Foxen Canyon Road to be used as a private residence.

Betteravia's Sugar Factory

HE OPENING OF THE SUGAR factory in Betteravia, overshadowed only by the discovery of oil on the Central Coast, brought a measure of prosperity to the farmers who had previously grown beans and barley, depending on good weather and the generosity of stores who carried them from season to season.

Ten years after Claud Spreckles of the Western Beet Sugar Company had come to look at property in the Santa Maria Valley and returned to San Francisco without making a commitment, a group of financiers and businessmen from San Francisco began to show an interest. Union Sugar Company incorporated on September 27, 1897.

With the necessary acreage, an abundance of water alongside in the historic Guadalupe Lake, and transportation and fuel supplies being attainable, everything that the company needed was located there.

Immediately after purchasing 4,000 acres of the Goldtree Tract in 1897, Union Sugar began to build its modern factory, with silos imported from Sweden, an endeavor that was destined to bring Santa Marians their first taste of prosperity. The factory went on to produce sugar for almost 100 years, becoming the country's longest continually operating factory. At one time it produced more sugar than any other sugar plant in the country.

The opening of the Union Sugar factory in September of 1899 marked a change in the local business scene and the beginning of industrial growth in the valley.

In addition to the Japanese contract workers who were brought in to work in the sugar beet fields, and later the Filipinos, the sugar factory hired people from Santa Maria and Guadalupe.

Guadalupe Lake, one of the deciding factors in convincing Union Sugar to build its factory here, was a naturally occurring lake that had once covered 1,000 acres. However, as the years passed and the water tables were greatly reduced because of increased agricultural and urban use, the lake became a storage basin for the water necessary in the processing of sugar.

Although the lake wasn't suitable for swimming, locals were able hunt ducks in the area. Later, according to Tim Thompson, the lake became "nothing but a bunch of brush with a little bit of water sitting at its base."

During the factory's heyday, rail cars carrying beets from around the state rumbled into Betteravia to drop off loads, dumping off almost 70 tons of beets per day for use in the processing of sugar that eventually sold under the names of Vons, Springfield, TV and their own label, Union Sugar. Liquid sugar for soft drinks or glaze for cookies was also processed at the factory.

About five years after the factory opened, the company began building houses for its employees, thus forming the town of Betteravia, the name taken from the French word *betterave,* meaning beet root. Approximately 70 two- and three-bedroom houses were built on three streets in back of the railroad tracks, with three or four blocks of houses to a street.

Although these streets had no official names, they were generally known as First, Second and

Third Streets.

Betteravia had just about everything that a person could want. With its own post office, grocery store, hotel, auditorium (where Audrey Silva, Santa Maria's famed woman of dance, came to give square dancing lessons), volunteer fire department, non-denominational church, park and a brick schoolhouse, the town had everything that it needed. During its earlier years, Doctor Dan Sink served as the town's physician.

Eight grades were taught in Betteravia's two-room red brick schoolhouse, with grades one through four being taught in one room and grades five through eight in the second room. Children who watched the blackboard and listened to the teacher as she instructed the higher grades could easily be double promoted. With from 32 to 38 children to each room, and the teacher giving individualized help, order was always maintained and the children received the highest quality education. The little school served the community well.

Thursdays at the school were reserved for the radio program, "The Standard Oil Symphony Hour," thus introducing the students to classical music, an interest that never waned. During the lunch hour, teacher Rose Cicero entertained the students by playing the piano. When the eighth grade students were ready to graduate and go on to Santa Maria High School, the awarding of diplomas by the Board of Trustees was always preceded by a class presentation of an operetta.

When Marilyn (Merkuris) Stanley, who grew up in the town of Betteravia, graduated from high school and took a temporary job with the Sugar Company by filling in for the office manager, her sights were set on attending Santa Maria Junior College (later Allan Hancock College). However, she wound up staying with the company and eventually became secretary to the company's vice president, a position that she held until she retired 43 years later.

One of the many pepper trees that the company planted to beautify the town stood outside the house of Dorothy and George Benford, who lived in Betteravia from 1953 to 1957.

The town's post office, located in Union Sugar's office building, opened for business as a fourth-class post office in 1897, with mail coming in by wagon from Santa Maria. When the local railroad built a spur out to Betteravia, mail came into town by rail.

Israel Martin Burola served as Betteravia's postmaster from 1900 to 1920. He also headed the company's merchandise store, which first served as a commissary

Union Sugar Company Factory, Betteravia, Cal. Sept. 29, 1924.

to furnish supplies to the hotel, boarding houses and to the surrounding ranchers. In 1904 the commissary became a general store, offering the hundreds of Japanese field workers a full line of imported Japanese food.

In 1936, when Pauline Pittori served as Postmistress, the government upgraded the Post Office classification to "third class."

Lillian Burrow retired from the town's Post Office two months before the office closed in 1970. After Mrs. Burrow's retirement, Elizabeth Muscio, who had worked there for 15 years, was appointed officer in charge and served in that capacity until the Post Office officially closed and the mail duties were taken over by rural carriers from Santa Maria.

The town's early fire department consisted of a two-wheel hand-drawn roller cart, a hose, and as many volunteers as could be rounded up. Finding volunteers was never a problem, though, as when the alarm sounded everyone ran out to fight the fire.

Louise Heitle, like Frank McCoy, who later opened the Santa Maria Inn, served as one of the managers of the 60-room Betteravia Hotel, which was located on a hill overlooking the lake. During World War II, the hotel was used to house military men and their families.

When the company decided to turn over the company's store operation to private entities in 1940, Bill (Tex) Wahrmund took it over and added a butcher shop. He also operated the town's gas station. The Wahrmunds lived in one unit of the four-apartment complex located southwest of the store. When they bought the J & J Market in Guadalupe, their connection with the town of Betteravia ended.

Jack and Lillian Burrow, who took over the Betteravia store in 1946, operated it for 22 years. Then, as in the store's earliest days, purchases that were charged were repaid from the employees'

monthly paychecks.

At the time the store closed in 1968, it had been the oldest continually operating single-location grocery store in the Santa Maria Valley.

The day that the sugar company decided to get out of the rental business marked the beginning of the end for the little town of Betteravia, and eventually, for the company itself.

By January of 1968, the hotel, boathouses, clubhouse, schools, stables and the wharf were all gone. Those who took advantage of the company's offer bought the houses for $50 and $75 and moved them to Simas Road (the back road to Guadalupe) and to Nipomo on $750 lots.

As the company bulldozed together the last eight houses and set them on fire, a group of former residents watched as silent witnesses as the town of Betteravia came to an end. The last buildings to go were the church and the firehouse, both scheduled to be demolished during the following year.

From the beginning, the Union Sugar factory, located "miles from nowhere," operated around the clock (except the period from 1927 to 1934, when a plant disease caused the factory to be shut down) and provided gainful employment to the people in the valley. For many, it was the only place where they had ever worked.

The historic Union Sugar Company was to know four owners. First known simply as the Union Sugar Company, the factory became known as Union Sugar, a division of Consolidated Foods Corporation, and later as Union Sugar, a division of Sara Lee Corporation. Finally, through a series of name changes, the factory became Imperial Holly Sugar.

After Holly Sugar took over the sugar factory in 1986, prices slipped to an all-time low. Transportation costs had increased, and government regulations had become more oppressive.

In May of 1993 the company announced to its

300 permanent and part-time employees that it would be closing its doors the following July, and that all but about 30 people would be let go. Although the factory would no longer be processing sugar beets, it would continue to store, package and distribute refined sugar products.

Twenty-five years after the town of Betteravia came to an end, the plant finally closed and the buildings started to come down one by one in November of 1996.

People who had once played parts in the running of the factory were now ghosts of its past. Alexander Merkuris, who had gone to work at the factory in 1920 and worked his way up to shift superintendent, retired in 1950. Ralph Rogers,

father of Helen Bishop, had served as plant superintendent around the turn of the century. Antonio Belloni, grandfather of Raymond "Speed" Alliani, had worked as plant custodian, riding out to the factory every day for 40 years in his horse-drawn buggy.

When the company and the town of Betteravia were finally demolished, a piece of shared history went with them. However, even though the factory was gone, the good working relationships and the close friendships that were developed and nurtured through the years were destined to last forever.

What Union Sugar gave to the valley is impossible to take away.

William T. Lucas, M.D.

E HAD THE REPUTATION of being as vigorous and blunt as he was kind and sympathetic, and was reported to be one of the most "consistently profane men in Santa Maria." Although he was known to say a whole sentence at a time without using a cuss word, "it didn't happen very often."

However, he was an excellent physician, one with deep feelings and responsibility for his many friends and patients. During the Spanish Flu epidemic of 1918, he worked around the clock, calling not only to check on his own patients, but stopping at various houses on the way home to ask if anyone was sick or needed his help.

William T. Lucas, the third oldest child of George Johnson and Sally Thomas Lucas, was born in Buchanan County, Missouri, in 1850. In May of 1864, the family pulled up stakes and traveled west with more than 60 covered wagons filled with friends and neighbors. In the latter part of September, after having been on the trail for four months, the pioneers arrived in Deer Lodge, Montana, where they took up land. From Montana, the Lucas family headed for Oregon, intending to settle there. However, after ten days of not seeing the sun, the family decided to move south, arriving in Woodland, California, in 1868.

Although his father was recognized as being the wagon leader, it is generally understood among family members that it was his mother who was the real leader. The elder Mrs. Lucas lived to be 96 years old, living her last years in Woodland.

William, always wanting to be a physician but lacking the necessary funds with which to attend medical school, attended Hesperian College in Woodland. When he first started to teach school in the town and his authority to teach was challenged by the school bully, he had to lick the upstart before he could continue teaching.

Lucas saved enough money to enroll in the University of the Pacific in San Francisco, where he graduated in 1876. In 1879, three years after becoming head of the Woodland Hospital, he and his wife, Lula, moved to the up-and-coming town of Guadalupe, where he set up his practice in the old adobe. It was here that their two children, Lee and Oreon ("Ora"), were born.

In 1882 he obtained an honorary degree from Cooper Medical College, now the medical department of Stanford University.

In 1884, after the narrow-gauge railroad ran its tracks through Santa Maria and his patients began to move to the growing town, so did the doctor.

Doctor Lucas was a lifetime member (and Past Master) of the Guadalupe Masonic Lodge. He was also a prominent member of the order itself, and was elected to the position of Grand Master of the Grand Lodge of California Masons in 1896. He was reputed to have had the most complete set of books on Masonry in the state, a collection that he was forced to replace twice because of destructive fires. At the time of his death in 1931, Doctor Lucas was the Dean of Grand Masters of Masons in the State of California.

Unknown to many of his patients, Doctor Lucas had a lifelong interest in education, and could read in both Greek and Latin. He was instrumental in organizing the Santa Maria Union High School and helping to make it one of the best schools in the state. He was also the first president of the Agricultural Association of the Santa Maria Valley.

During his early years in the area, the doctor made his house calls with a horse and buggy. More often than not, though, by the time he reached the house of a patient, it was too late for him to head back to his home, so he spent the night there, keeping an eye on his patient during the night.

William Lucas "Bill" Blanckenburg, grandson of Doctor Lucas, remembered taking the train from Berkeley to visit his grandfather in Santa Maria every summer. During one such visit, when young Bill came down with the measles, the doctor, knowing that his daughter was a member of the Christian Science faith, went to the house of a local practitioner, insisting that she come with him to treat his grandson. The woman, caught by surprise, felt uncomfortable at the thought of going to a doctor's home, and said that she'd give the boy treatment in absence. "The hell you will!" he roared. "You get over there! I want to see how it's done!"

Doctor Lucas maintained his office and residence in a two-story building on the northeast corner of Chapel and Vine streets, an office that he shared with Doctors Zach and Bert Coblentz. Their father, Samuel Coblentz, and his friend and partner, L. M. Schwabacher, were popular merchants in town. Years later, Bill Coblentz, son of Zach, served as Deputy Attorney General for the State of California and was appointed to the University of California Board of Regents, a position that he held from 1964 to 1980.

When young Bill Blanckenburg made his annual visits to his grandfather, his mother worried and prayed a lot. When Bill accompanied his grandfather on his rounds, the boy prayed, too.

By this time, Doctor Lucas was driving a Model T Ford, a machine that he despised.

Life had been less complicated when he was driving his horse and buggy, as he could focus his mind on the treatment of his patients instead of maneuvering the confounded foot pedals. "When I'm driving I have my mind on other things!"

He had a carpenter install a door at each end of his garage to protect the back wall. This also served a more useful purpose. Because he didn't like to back up—foot pedal problems again—the double opening enabled him to drive forward out into his field, turn around, head back into the garage and then out onto the street.

Every morning he visited his favorite tavern on Whiskey Row and had the bartender fill his daily order of a glass of bourbon and a raw egg. The doctor liked his liquor, but never let it interfere with his medical practice.

Never opposed to the use of profanity, he was

once seen running after his car yelling, "Whoa! You S.O.B.!" (Of course, the kindly doctor wasn't inclined to use initials.)

Blanckenburg remembered a rabies epidemic in the area when all dogs seen on the street were subject to being shot. Doctor Lucas, who was the health officer at the time, carried a loaded Smith & Wesson on the seat beside him. He assured his grandson, who sat next to him in the passenger seat, that he was a crack shot after having shot many rabbits while living in Montana. However, as far as his grandson remembered, the gun was never used.

In addition to a little house on the property that the doctor rented out, there was also a tank house occupied by a man named Jack Coffey. Coffey, who lived on the property for many years rent-free, did odd jobs for the doctor in exchange for free rent. The man, according to Blanckenburg, didn't have much use for the doctor, but accepted his rent-free status. Doctor Lucas didn't seem to mind the arrangement. "Where would he go from here?" was his philosophy.

The doctor began his day by eating garlic and taking a cold bath, two rituals that he practiced every day of his life. While staying at the Palace Hotel in San Francisco when the big earthquake struck in the early morning hours, he jumped out of bed to extract the last drop of cold water for his bath before going down to offer his help.

Like many country doctors, Dr. Lucas accepted produce in lieu of cash, and when a patient died, he wrote on the ledger, "Paid by God."

Like many professional people of his time, he wasn't much of a businessman. Unlike many local people who grew wealthy at the time, the doctor's investments in oil exploration projects never paid off.

At the time of his death in 1931, the doctor's estate was estimated to be $50,000, with real estate valuations and cash on hand taken into account. One of his properties was an 80-acre parcel of land located near Santa Maria Way and the 101 Freeway. Some time after the doctor's death, the Santa Maria Way property was sold off as three parcels, one of which was sold to Doctor Ikola. Another parcel of property was located out where the old golf course was located in Orcutt on the road to Vandenberg.

Although Doctor and Mrs. Lucas separated in 1903, the couple never divorced. She went to live in Berkeley in a house that the doctor had built for her. She lived on one side of the flat while the Blanckenburgs lived on the other side. Lula Lucas passed away in 1937. As a member of the Maupin family, she too came from early pioneer stock.

Of the three Blanckenburg grandchildren, Bill (affectionately called "William the Silent" by his grandfather) served 18 years as an attorney and 22 years as a Superior Court Judge in Napa County. Ted ("the Terrible") graduated from the California Maritime Academy and served as a Merchant Marine Captain at sea. He took time out to attend law school and became an attorney, but he much preferred his life at sea. Ted met a violent death in 1972 when only 52 years of age. Betty ("the Better") lived in the Southern California.

Although Dr. Lucas eventually gave up his extensive practice, he acted in an advisory capacity at the clinic for a number of years and assisted in numerous cases. However, he was always ready, day or night, when an old friend needed him

Santa Maria's own Doctor Lucas, the man who "delivered 3,000 babies and never lost a mother," died of pneumonia in 1931 at the age of 81.

Honorary pallbearers at the service for this pioneer physician, good friend and fraternal leader included Samuel Coblentz, L. M. Schwabacher, Leopold Scaroni, George M. Scott, Edward Rubel, L. J. Morris, Elvezio Righetti, Paul Tietzen, A. J. Souza, William H. Rice, William H. Tunnell, T. R. Finley, Ulisse Tognazzini and A. R. Jones.

The Los Alamos Earthquake

RIOR TO THE MONTH OF JULY in 1902, Los Alamos was typical of the growing, bustling little towns on the Central Coast.

The Wickenden Brothers operated a general store surrounded by a wooden platform sidewalk on the corner of Centennial and Main Streets. Fred Kriegel operated a butcher shop in a building that was owned by John Bell, who, along with Doctor James Barron Shaw, had founded the town of Los Alamos in 1876.

It wasn't long before the town had a church and a schoolhouse. Later, when the post office was built, Alexander Leslie became its first postmaster as well as the town's notary public and insurance agent. Jack Snyder, agent for Wells Fargo Express Company, opened the Union Hotel, and the Laughlin brothers ran a general merchandise store.

The town had two blacksmith shops, a livery stable and a flour mill, while Bert Laughlin operated the town's only drug store. Twenty-three-year-old John Richard Wickenden, youngest son of Frederick and Ramona Wickenden, acted as night watchman at the Wickenden Brothers Store and occupied a room inside the store.

Although residents of the little town were concerned about the weeks of rumbling beneath the ground, not many of them put much stock in the earthquake predictions of the old timers . . . that is, until the night of July 27, when a sudden jolt threw the sleepy residents from their beds. With the exception of a few toppled chimneys and many frayed nerves, the town stayed pretty much intact until the following Thursday, July 31, at 1:20 a.m., when the granddaddy of them all hit the sleepy town.

Those who were awake at the time remembered feeling the earth beginning to rise, tremble, rock and twist before giving a sudden, violent jolt which threw the townspeople from their beds. The frightened people ran outside, huddled together and prayed in the dark while the town seemed to collapse around them.

Windows were smashed, and everything made of brick toppled to the ground. At the crack of dawn, when darkness began to fade away, the people were able to assess the damage. The shaking continued for days. The Kriegels, afraid that their house was going to fall down on top of them, slept in their garden for a year.

When a rumor spread that the president of the University of California advised the residents to leave town "at the earliest possibility," about 60 of the town's 500 residents evacuated the area, only to return sheepishly a few days later. It was later reported that the president of the university was on vacation and hadn't even been in the area at the time.

The after-shocks continued until the following December, with newspapers having a field day printing so-called "first-hand" reports which later proved to be untrue.

When the clean-up and rebuilding began, many of the merchants, after assessing the damage done to their stores, decided to leave the area. Fred and Robert Wickenden stayed in the town for about two more years before moving to San Luis Obispo, where they opened a hardware store, while their brother Dick stayed and eventually took over the family's ranch operation. 🪶

Fire!

N ADDITION TO the red spiders, wild horses and jackrabbits bent on challenging their survival, early Valley homesteaders had to contend with roaring prairie fires, which, aided by notorious gale winds, threatened their very existence.

Between 1867 and 1869, three prairie fires sent flames high into the sky as they came roaring and crackling through the Valley, forcing wild animals to flee before them.

As more settlers arrived in the valley, the prairie fires abated. However, since most of the early business buildings were built close together and were nothing more than matchboxes with cloth and paper linings, once a fire started, the fire brigades could do little more than pass the buckets from man to man and hope for the best. Mostly, though, they chose to let the burning buildings be consumed by the fire while they concentrated on trying to save the nearby structures.

The T. A. Jones building on Broadway was the major building lost in the fire of 1883. The fire of 1884, for many years considered the "big fire," took with it every building on the northeast block of Main Street with the exception of the Odd Fellows Hall.

With no fire safety measures, no fire equipment and no organized firefighting skills, buildings didn't stand much of a chance. Those merchants who had sufficient financial means put up brick buildings.

On January 11, 1900, when the sounds of pealing church bells awakened the city to the fury of a major fire in its midst, the usual bucket brigade was formed to fight an out-of-control fire at the Santa Maria Hotel. The chemical engine, which had long been standing idle, was brought out and the fire was finally extinguished. The people, realizing the value of brick walls, fireproof buildings and an ample supply of water, finally conceded that it was time for a change.

In 1904 Arthur S. MacLaughlin set up the first organized fire department, with Henry Yelkin, Isaac Miller, Jr., Lindsay McMillan, Al Bunce, Ben Miller, Frank Jessee and George Brown serving as volunteer firemen.

When a used touring car was purchased from the Union Sugar Company, the mechanical expertise of W. H. Crakes and his two brothers, Frank and Clarence, enabled the chassis to be lengthened two feet, thus creating the foundation of Santa Maria's first fire truck. When the job was completed, the truck had a hose bed along with 1,000 feet of hose, two ladders, axes, lanterns, a pike pole and a 40-gallon tank for water.

Although the truck didn't contain a fire pump for boosting pressure, it was a great improvement over the hand-drawn hose cart that was being stored near the jail on Miller Street.

When MacLaughlin left the department, Dean Laughlin took over the helm, earning a salary of $20 per month.

In 1917, a new pumping engine, purchased from the American LaFrance Company, was unloaded and brought to Santa Maria from Guadalupe. As fate would have it, the first fire that the pumper was called out on was in Guadalupe!

Fire at the Santa Maria Fire Station, 1956

When Dean Laughlin retired in 1920, Frank Crakes was promoted from Assistant Chief to Chief. His brother Bill became Assistant Chief, with another brother, Clarence, serving as a volunteer fireman.

Although church bells were the first fire alarm system, a steam whistle at the water plant was later used as a fire alarm until an official siren replaced it in 1915.

Soon after World War I, the Gas Company, which owned the building on North Lincoln where the fire department headquarters was located, reclaimed the property, and the fire department was moved to a building owned by Albert A. Dudley in the 200 block of South Lincoln.

After construction was begun on a new site adjoining City Hall and the siren was mounted on top of the tank tower at the water plant, the city began to purchase more up-to-date fire equipment.

Then came the notorious fire of 1956.

The city's fire station had been built in 1937 for a total cost of $17,000. The fire department consisted of three paid firemen plus any number of volunteers who happened to show up when the siren sounded.

On the morning of the 25th of May, a fire, apparently caused by gas leaking from one of the fire trucks, ignited a blaze that was destined to bring Santa Maria national news coverage.

The fireman on duty, Raymond Smith, was there alone when the fire started. With his pant leg on fire and a burned hand, he tried to douse both the blaze and his burning trousers. However, the station fire had gotten out of hand. When he attempted to sound the fire alarm and found that the siren had shorted out, he raced to the City Administrator's office and shouted for someone to call the police. The office staff contacted the Water Department, who turned on an old World War II air raid alarm, calling for help.

Fire at the Santa Maria Fire Station, 1956

In the meantime, an observant crossing guard ran into the police station to report seeing smoke and flames pouring out from beneath the doors of the fire station.

Volunteers, brought out by the screeching alarm, arrived at the blazing building ready to attack the flames with fire hoses. However, the fire hoses were all inside the building and were being consumed by the fire.

After calls for help were made to the surround-

ing towns, fire trucks began to roll in from Guadalupe, Lompoc, Orcutt, Nipomo and the County station at the Santa Maria Airport. By the time they arrived, though, it was too late to save the building and the fire trucks parked inside.

When the fire was finally out, the smoking wrecks of the fire engines were pulled out onto the driveway, and cameras began to click.

When an assessment of the fire was made, the city announced that although the building, ladders and equipment were covered by insurance, the three trucks that had been destroyed by the fire were not.

News of the fire at the fire station spread like wildfire. Even *Life* magazine ran the story, complete with a picture of the three burned-out engines parked in front of what remained of the fire station.

A new fire station was built across the street at a cost of $50,000.

Many changes have been made since the fire of 1956. The Santa Maria Fire Department, in battling fires of different origins, has built a reputation of producing well-trained and professional personnel not only to fight the city's fires, but also to provide ongoing education to the public regarding fire prevention and safety. 🔥

The Carnegie Library

HEN THE CARNEGIE FAMILY left Scotland for New York in 1848 and settled in Allegheny, Pennsylvania, Andrew Carnegie was thirteen years old. Fifty-two years later, after selling his Carnegie Steel Mill in Pittsburgh to J. P. Morgan, he devoted the rest of his life to philanthropic pursuits, one of which was the funding of Carnegie Libraries throughout the English-speaking world.

Possibly remembering the days when he didn't have the $2 subscription fee with which to borrow books from the country's first libraries, Carnegie began promoting the free library idea at a time when there were few libraries in the entire world. The man who was later referred to as the "Patron Saint of Public Libraries" made it his goal to make books available to everyone in his adopted country. By the time that his library-funding program was terminated in 1917, 1681 Carnegie Libraries had been built in the United States, with the majority located in small towns. Andrew Carnegie died two years later, three months short of reaching his 84th birthday.

The building of the Carnegie Library in Santa Maria was accomplished through the diligent work of the Minerva Library Club (later to become The Minerva Club).

The story of the Library Club goes back to 1894, when 25 women, wanting to feed their knowledge and to make the town a better place in which to live, gathered at the home of Mollie Smith. To accomplish their goals, the women of the newly organized "Ladies Literary Society" pledged to donate their time and talents to the success of their new organization.

During the following years Santa Marians were provided with culture usually found only in the big cities.

In March of 1896 a committee was formed to find a home for the group's circulating library. This library was destined to see many homes, including the reception room of a dental office, and the lobby of the Post Office (then located on the west side of Broadway, between Main and Church Streets, in the Jones Building).

By 1899 the women had a thriving adult-serving library of 268 books and were able to pay a Literary Society member $1 a month for services as librarian. Four years later she received a $1 raise in pay.

In 1901, when the ladies felt that it was time for the city to have a community library, they sent the first of many letters to Andrew Carnegie.

Although the women felt that a library would one day be built and were in the process of buying property on the northwest corner of Cook and Broadway to house it, negotiations with Mr. Carnegie proved to be slow.

Carnegie wound up approving the building of the library on city property on the 400 block of South Broadway, rather than the club's property across the street. However, the ladies were ecstatic in knowing that Santa Maria would soon have a library.

Mr. Carnegie, always cost-conscious, insisted that although he would donate $10,000 ("and not a penny more"), the city would first have to fund the remaining costs before he'd donate a dime. James F. Goodwin opened with a $500 subscription, and others soon followed until Carnegie's requirement was met.

Carnegie also specified that his money was to be used only for the actual building, and that receipts from the contractor must be presented to him for approval. He would then make payments in installments.

The need to make variations in the original plans was apparent. Although the original Carnegie plans called for an unfinished basement, the trustees decided to finish it at an added cost of $400. Cement walks, gas fixtures and grading problems escalated the costs to much more than Carnegie's $10,000 donation. The difference, of course, had to be paid through city sources.

In addition to his funding specifications, Mr. Carnegie stipulated that the building must face the city's most prominent street, the land could only be used as a library or a park, and the City Council would have to agree to maintain the library for permanent public use.

Actual construction began on the library in early August of 1908, when the city treasurer, William A. Haslam, announced that contractor Frank Darby had submitted the lowest bid. After Darby completed the construction in May of the following year, and the Minerva Club donated 600 books, a special room in the building was appropriated for the club's use in appreciation for all that the women had done.

Lazarus Blochman, using his personal funds, landscaped the property and purchased the trees surrounding the building. The following year the city assumed responsibility for the care of the grounds.

Mrs. Minnie Stearns, an artist and former teacher, became head librarian at a salary of $70 per month for "librarian and janitorial services." The city, never free with its money, decided not to send Mrs. Stearns to a San Diego conference in 1914. Instead, she was given a two-week vacation so that she could attend the conference at her own expense. Mrs. Stearns' wages remained the same until 1924, when the City Council voted to increase her salary to $110.

When Mrs. Stearns retired in 1934 after 25 years of service, her staff included two full-time assistants, a part-time employee, plus a "page" (a young girl who worked without pay in order to learn the library business). Dorothea Dudley, later to marry Paul Nelson, succeeded Mrs. Stearns as head librarian.

Shortly after the Carnegie building was completed, a hexagon bandstand, at a cost of $1,000, was constructed south of the building, where the Santa Maria Band gave weekly concerts.

The stately Carnegie Library, with its high steps and lofty columns duplicating other Carnegie Libraries dotting the country at that time, served Santa Maria for almost 60 years.

In November of 1939, after determining that the old relic was unable to meet the needs of the growing population, the City Council ordered architects Crawford and Davis to draw up plans for a new library to harmonize with City Hall in the style of California Spanish Missions. H. E. Small was hired as contractor.

The new Santa Maria Library, costing $36,700, was one of the last libraries built on the West Coast until the war ended in 1945. It was dedicated on July 15, 1941.

Through the years the old library building was used for many purposes, including USO entertainment and City Council meetings. Eventually, when the building had stood vacant for some length of time, members of the City Council, determining that rehabilitation would be too costly, voted to demolish the building.

The wood-and-brick building, one of the most beautiful and visited edifices on the Central Coast area in its time, was torn down in August of 1966.

No one seems to know what the name of this team was, but it proudly bears the Santa Maria moniker. Standing, left to right: Billy Miles, 3rd base; T. Miller, 1st base; Boone DeWitt, outfielder; George "Don" Merritt, pitcher; Haight Jessee, 2nd base. Middle row, left to right: R. O. "Bob" Walker of Orcutt, outfielder; George Brown, umpire; Isaac Miller, pitcher. Sitting, left to right: Henry Morris, outfielder; Frank Jessee, catcher; Herschel Miller, shortstop.

Baseball in Santa Maria

EGEND SAYS that when U.S. Army volunteers arrived in Santa Barbara in 1847 to help colonize the recently acquired territory, they brought with them the newly invented game of baseball. Instead of being impressed, the Californianos were certain that these Americanos were crazy.

When the game of baseball was introduced to the Santa Maria Valley in 1882, it quickly caught on. Before long each town had its own baseball team, with people of every age wanting to get into the game. However, when some of those who were less agile than others went home with mashed fingers, disjointed thumbs and, in some cases, dislocated jaws, they soon settled for just being cheering spectators. This game of baseball was serious business best left to the younger guys.

A playing field was created when level land was cleared off, a makeshift backstop was set up, and four bags to be used as bases were set down. The team was then ready to "play ball."

Each oil lease supported baseball teams where the competition was fierce.

In the spring of 1882, when both the Santa Maria Stars and their arch-rivals in Guadalupe had their eyes set on winning the championship belt and silver-mounted ball, the Stars wound up winning the hotly-contested competition of skills.

Around the turn of the 20th century, the A. Flasher Company, a business then located on the corner of Broadway and East Main Street, sponsored a team that was destined to win the hearts and affections of the local fans.

Fred Lewis from the Santa Maria Bottling Works was the team's official umpire, with Frank Jessee serving as manager. The players included Roscoe Jones, Roy Sherman, Dr. Blosser, Johnny Avila, Mike Price, George Miller, Joe Fisher and Henry Bunce.

Joe Fisher was the team's captain, Mike Price was the pitcher, and Johnny Avila the catcher. Jessee looked after the business end while the rest of the players cavorted around the bases at the old racetrack.

The powerful A.F. Company team played and defeated teams from as far north as San Luis Obispo and as far south as Ventura. On one memorable occasion the team played a double header on home territory and won both games.

Enthusiasm grew in proportion to the team's success, and before the season was over, everyone in town was wild about its team, the attendance was large, and betting was open and above board.

Henry Bunce, one of the earnest, hard-working wonders of the team, worked for the Pacific Coast Railway for many years

In 1907, the young men of Santa Maria formed the "Golden Bears" Club, a single men's club. With Fred Haslam as manager, the team, complete with uniforms for each man, was made up of the Langlois Brothers, Landon Bagby, Elwood Bryant, Emmett Trott, Archie Cline, Elmer Boyd, Dick Doane, Bert Smith, Bert Jessee, Lee Brown, Nelson Jones and Fred Haslam.

Through the years the Valley has supported baseball teams that played against any team that wanted to play the game.

Through the coaching of "Kit" Carson of Santa Maria High School, the Saints won nine championships in a row from 1930 to 1939. In 1932, the team beat the Herbert Hoover High School team to win the CIF Championship.

In 1939 Cappy Harada was one of 5 Japanese players on the high school's team. After World War II ended, General Douglas MacArthur appointed him to the job of reviving professional and college sports in Japan.

In 1944 Santa Maria's semi-professional Indians team was formed. Mutt Anderson, who had played catcher with the Santa Maria Valley Railroad's team and later with a Canadian league, came aboard as the new team's first manager.

Through the years Santa Marians have given unending support to the Indians, and have not only seen the team compete in the semi-professional World Series in Wichita, Kansas, but have seen a number of players go on to the big leagues, beginning with Les Webber, who signed with the Brooklyn Dodgers in 1941. Since that time such major league teams as the Cleveland Indians, the Cincinnati Reds, the San Diego Padres, the St. Louis Cardinals, the Boston Red Sox, the Toronto Blue Jays, the California Angels, the Milwaukee Brewers, the New York Mets, the Chicago White Sox, the New York Yankees, the Detroit Tigers, the Los Angeles Dodgers, and the Seattle Mariners have all drawn from the ranks of the Santa Maria Indians.

Other prominent names in the history of the Indians included Butch Simas, one of the original founders of the Tribe, who served as Manager and President of the team from 1945 to 1960. Mr. Simas passed away in 1990. Joe Hagerman gave unending support to the Indians from the time of its inception.

Scoop Nunes, Santa Maria's "Mr. Baseball," was inducted into the National Semi-Professional Baseball Hall of Fame in Wichita, Kansas, in August of 1977 and the Santa Maria Hall of Fame in January of 1993. 🎽

The Paulding Family

F THE FOUR PAULDING brothers who came to the Central Coast in the 1880s, three were in the medical field, while the fourth brother, Mel, was a farmer. A fifth brother, James, was a policeman in Ohio. The brothers had three sisters, Sarah, Christina and Mary.

Although both Doctors Edwin and Ormond Paulding were born in Damascus, Syria, where their father, Joseph Gardner Paulding was a medical missionary, Will was born in the family home in Ohio.

When Edwin Paulding, who was the first of the Pauldings to come to the Central Coast, came through Arroyo Grande on his way to visit a friend in Los Olivos, he was so impressed by the many pumpkins he saw, that he decided that this was the place where he wanted to settle. He returned to Ohio, picked up his belongings, and returned to Arroyo Grande, arriving there in 1883.

Before two years had passed, both Will and Ormond arrived, and the three went into business together, with Will, the pharmacist, filling prescriptions for his brothers' patients.

Some years later, when Mary Paulding, daughter of Ormond and Flora Paulding, related her family's history, she said that her parents had come to California in a tiny buggy which they used in camping out along the way. They wound up selling the wagon and coming the rest of the way by train.

Mary Lola Paulding and her twin sister Christina Litti Paulding were born August 28, 1887, at the family home on Cherry Street in Arroyo Grande.

Both Will and Ormond were amateur photographers, while Edwin's hobby was woodworking. Will was said to have been the most sports-minded of the three, and was always the first to test the waters when the fishing season opened.

However, the brothers couldn't get along, and they were often on the verge of breaking up.

Dr. Ormond Paulding eventually left Arroyo Grande and went to Andersen, California, and later to Templeton, before coming to Santa Maria in 1892 to buy Dr. Snow's medical practice.

For recreation, Ormond and Flora Paulding often piled their daughters into their Democrat Wagon and took them to the Pismo Beach tent city. Because Dr. Edwin refused to allow his family to celebrate Christmas, all of the brothers and their families would gather at his house on Thanksgiving. Although Edwin was a Seventh-day Adventist and didn't permit his family to eat meat, he did permit them to eat turkey on Thanksgiving.

Even as a child, Mary played the part of a nurse and often practiced her skills by bandaging up the neighborhood children as well as any animal that happened to come her way. She took her nurse's training at General Hospital in Los Angeles, where she spent eight hours working on the floor with no pay, doing whatever work was assigned to her in this "working hospital." When her workday ended, she spent an additional four hours in classroom study.

After receiving her nurse's cap on February 23, 1911, she returned to Santa Maria, where she went out with her father on house calls to his many patients. Many times she stayed at the home of a patient for two or three weeks, not only helping the patient to recuperate, but also doing light housekeeping and helping with the cooking.

From April to August of 1918, Mary took her Army training at the Letterman Hospital at the San Francisco Presidio; in September, she was sent overseas to the war front in France, where she spent several months working at the Evacuation Hospital on the Meuse - Argonne Front—a tent hospital much like the one in *M*A*S*H*. She came home in March of 1919 and was discharged the following month on disability. As far as anyone knew, Mary had no disability; however, by this time she was 32 years old, and it's possible that she was considered to be too old for the Army.

After coming home from the war, she continued home nursing, and even worked at the nurses' station during the 1923 filming of Cecil B. DeMille's *The Ten Command-*

ments in the Guadalupe Dunes. In the 1930s she worked with some of the first polio patients at Mrs. Gregory's Santa Maria County Hospital, where part of the treatment was placing the patients into an iron lung. Mary would spend hours rubbing the patients' arms and legs, trying to restore circulation. At the end of the day, all employees at the hospital bathed, changed clothes, and left their work clothes at the hospital before returning to their homes.

During the construction of Vandenberg Air Force Base, Mary worked at the nurses' station for construction workers. In her last years of nursing, she did private duty work at the Sisters Hospital in Santa Maria.

After World War I, Mary lived at 119 West Cook Street with her parents and sister Ormonde ("Ormie"), who worked for 35 years at the Santa Maria Post Office. Her twin sister Litti, who had once taught in the Santa Maria school system, went to work for the *Santa Barbara News-Press,* where she eventually became the paper's society editor.

Mary had a gruff side, except when caring for her patients.

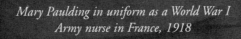

Mary Paulding in uniform as a World War I
Army nurse in France, 1918

Her genuine caring exceeded her impeccable professional image. Whenever a person took sick, the word was put out to "Get Mary!"

She was an active lifelong member of Santa Maria's American Legion Post 56, and she attended many of the national conventions as a representative of the local post.

In 1972, Mary moved to Hanford to be near Litti and another relative, Nancy. Ormonde had died of lung cancer in the 1950s. When the two sisters became too sick to take care of themselves, they entered a nursing home, where Mary passed away in 1976 at the age of 88. Litti died a month later.

Dr. Ormond Pinkerton Paulding, his wife and their three daughters are buried in the Santa Maria Cemetery.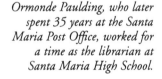

Ormonde Paulding, who later spent 35 years at the Santa Maria Post Office, worked for a time as the librarian at Santa Maria High School.

The Swiss-Italians

HE HISTORY OF THE Swiss-Italians in the Santa Maria Valley is one of incredibly hard work and perseverance. Many of those who had gone first to the diamond mines of South America and Australia later came to California to try their luck in the gold mines.

The Swiss-Italians who had come to California from the canton of Ticino in Switzerland had come to the United States by any means available, often spending 14 long days on the ocean and even more time in crossing the United States.

During the middle 1860s, those who hadn't found luck in the gold mines moved down to Cayucos, Petaluma and Greenfield, where they began dairy farming. At the turn of the century, the Salinas Valley became the site of the largest Swiss-Italian community in the United States.

Some of the farmers, after learning of the year-round growing season in the Santa Maria Valley, headed south just about when the Rancho Guadalupe was being subdivided by Theodore LeRoy.

Antonio Pietra Tognazzini was the first Swiss-Italian to arrive in Guadalupe from Cayucos. In 1876 he purchased 497 acres of the Green Canyon Ranch for $22 an acre. The following year, he married Lucia LaFranchi of Cayucos, and the couple had three sons, Joseph, Pizziero and Romildo. Twelve years after purchasing the land, Antonio returned to Switzerland, where he passed away in 1922.

Joseph Tognazzini, eldest son of Antonio and Lucia, was born in 1879 and attended Laguna School, then located on Point Sal Road. He was ten years old when he returned to Switzerland with his parents. In 1906 he married Lia Dalidio, and the couple had six children.

Arturo, the second son of Joseph and Lia, migrated to this country in 1928 and went to work for his uncle Romildo on his one-third portion of the Green Canyon Ranch. In 1936, Arturo took over his father's ownership of the ranch and operated a dairy.

Battista Pezzoni, who arrived in 1876 from Someo, went into partnership with Giuseppe Muscio and Valerio Tognazzini in purchasing 8000 acres of land near Los Alamos to use for cattle grazing.

Seventeen-year-old Lillie Mae, the Pezzonis' first child, married Elvezio Righetti in a service performed by W. E. Stokes in January of 1894. Righetti, also from Someo, had come to California by way of Panama, landing in Cayucos in 1867. During the 1880s he followed many of his countrymen in coming to the Santa Maria Valley and opening a dairy. The Righettis had seven children, Alfred, Edith, Ernest, Tilden, Leo, Lillian and Paul.

Ernest Elvezio Righetti married Anna Adeline Oakley, daughter of Cary Calvin and Mary Oakley. The couple had two children, Ernest II and Anadelle.

In 1962, in commemorating Righetti's 70 continuous years of service to the schools in the Santa Maria Valley, the high school district named its newest school the Ernest Righetti High School.

Most of the Swiss-Italian immigrants established farms in the western end of the valley, where the climate was ideal for dairy cattle. Accustomed to life in a republic, they had no problem in adjusting to the rugged life on their dairy farms where the work was hard and the days were long. However, almost without exception, they prospered.

After crossing the country by railroad to San Francisco and then down to San Luis Obispo, Peter Ferini came to Guadalupe in 1882 to join his brother Carlo, and the two worked on the Pezzoni dairy farm. When Paul Tietzen, head cashier at the Bank of Santa Maria, approached Peter in 1902 to tell him that the Davy Brown property was about to be put up for sale, Ferini purchased the property. Thinking that he might have gotten in over his head, Ferini sold 50 acres to a man by the name of Moretti, from Switzerland, and leased his newly acquired property to Union Sugar for ten years.

In 1904, Peter Ferini married Irene Coppi, a young woman who had come to California with Mrs. Pezzoni.

In 1922, Ferini, who had been living in San Luis Obispo County, returned to his Guadalupe property, where he set up a dairy farm. The Ferinis eventually gave up dairy farming, and in 1929 began farming, raising cauliflower, broccoli and celery.

By the time 15-year-old Joe Stornetta arrived in Guadalupe in 1910 to join his brother, Henry, there were many Swiss-Italians living in the town, and young Joe fit right in. He attended the Laguna School in Guadalupe before going to Pomona three years later to work for his uncle. While there, he attended Pomona Business College. When he returned to Guadalupe, he found a position with the Guadalupe Bank, and also worked a season with the Union Sugar Company. In 1917 he enlisted in the U. S. Army and was honorably discharged in 1919, receiving

The Stornetta brothers, 1926:
Louis, Ralph, Joseph and Lawrence.

Righetti had served on the Boards of Trustees of the Orcutt Union Grammar School District, the Santa Maria Union High School District and Junior College, the Santa Maria Joint Union High School District, and Allan Hancock College. Righetti was also a Director of the Bank of America. Ernest Righetti II was a Founder and Director of the Community Bank of Santa Maria.

citizenship in return for his service. He became a charter member of the Santa Maria post of the American Legion.

In addition to working at his uncle's dairy, Stornetta and his brothers operated the Speed Ranch dairy farm, where they kept 120 cows on 160 acres. He later married Julia Martines. When the Great Depression came and hard times fell on the country, Stornetta lost most of his property.

In February of 1933 Stornetta moved his family to the Twitchell Ranch (where Kmart is now located) and began raising cattle and pigs.

The DeBernardis came to area in the mid-1930s and eventually opened a dairy on East Main Street.

All of the dairies, with the exception of DeBernardi's, are gone. The descendants of these early Swiss pioneers, in pursuing other endeavors, have become bankers, lawyers, teachers, or insurance brokers, and are listed in a host of other professions.

Without a doubt, the Swiss-Italian pioneers have contributed much to the valley. With each one playing his part in adding another chapter to the story of the Santa Maria Valley, such names as Stornetta, Tognazzini, Caroni, Albertoni, Giacomini, Minetti, Maretti, Ferini, Bassi, Bonetti, Bondietti, Ferrari, Sutti, Pezzoni, Dolcini, Righetti, Diani, Freddi, LaFranchi and many others reflect a history of incredibly hard work and determination that was so prevalent in our pioneers. 🕉

The Last Vaquero

HEN LEANDRO CASTRO, son of Simon and Sara Castro, showed up for work at the Suey Ranch in 1912, the other vaqueros didn't pay him much attention. However, it didn't take long for them to see that they had someone special in their midst when his superb performance in rodeos set them all back on their heels. He always walked away with all of the prizes in bulldogging, calf roping and team roping, and was second to none in the breaking of wild horses. In the world of hard-riding vaqueros, Leandro Castro proved to be the best of the best.

Leandro Malathón (Milton) Castro was born on March 10, 1885, in Jolon, California, and was baptized three days later in the Mission San Miguel Arcangel. At the age of thirteen, he ran away from home and landed a job in a gold mine near Jolon. Although the work was hard, he stuck it out.

When sickness overcame the boy, William Mayo Newhall found him and took him under his wing, providing him with the best of medical care until he was once again well and strong.

After listening to the boy's pleas not to be sent back to his parents, Newhall sent Leandro to work as a sheepherder on his Piojo Ranch (later to become the Hunter-Liggett Military Reservation). The ranch was later sold to William Randolph Hearst.

It was during his tenure at the Piojo that the boy had his first experience in riding horses. While driving cattle from the ranch to the company's Suey Rancho, just northeast of Santa Maria, his favorite stopping-off place was Santa

Margarita, where his arrival was always celebrated with a dance.

After being transferred to the Suey Rancho in 1912, Castro's reputation as an all-around cowboy soared.

In the days before a cement bridge was built over the Suey crossing of the Santa Maria River, any heavy storm brought torrential floods to the area. An inundation of water, logs, branches and other debris from the mountains would come tearing down the river, making it impossible for people to cross. The river's water often overflowed into the city of Santa Maria, sometimes deluging the land as far south as Fesler Street.

Although the extreme height of the flow didn't last long after the storm was over, there remained a wide and treacherous stream for a long period of time, and the quicksand and uncharted deep holes made crossing the river a hazardous undertaking.

Those needing transportation across the river came to depend on Leandro Castro, who directed other vaqueros from the Suey and drove stakes with flags of red cloth to show the safest and most shallow path from bank to bank. Soon it became a challenge to see who could be first to run his horse into the river while carrying the guiding rope to riders behind, and plunge his stake into the ground. Of course, Castro always won.

Although Castro was called in the last draft of World War I, he was just getting on the train in San Luis Obispo to report for duty when the signing of the Armistice was announced. He returned to his work, and on the 27th of December that year, he and Mary Alice Braffet were married.

Castro was also an avid bullfighter, having thrilled crowds in Mexico City as well as in Paso Robles and King City before the sport was outlawed in this country.

A man steeped in the life of the open, Castro was also an expert in the ancient Spanish art of weaving intricate quirts and of making ropes and *riatas* of horsehair. Those pieces of art, made by a man who could easily be called "a man's man," have been handed down to his descendants.

Leandro Malathón Castro lived through a time of change. The man who once drove cattle down long dusty roads into town for shipment to market lived to see them driven up the ramps of huge trucks and transported down the highway, headed for the stockyards.

This trustworthy all-around cowboy, Santa Maria's own, who came from a time when a man's handshake was his word, lived through and was part of the fascination and color of a California long since gone.

Leandro Castro passed away on April 10, 1954. 🐾

Ellen Peterson Kortner Tunnell

I N September of 1884, four-year-old Ellen Peterson left Denmark with her mother and brother Jim and set sail for the United States to join her father, Peter, who was working on his uncle's farm in the Nipomo area. Her sister, Marie, who was considered too frail to make the long voyage, stayed with her maternal grandparents until she turned 18 and the Germans, who controlled Denmark at the time, feeling that she was old enough to be on her own, ordered her out of the country.

After the family was settled in Nipomo, another child, Rasmus, was born. Peter passed away shortly afterwards.

About this time, Christian Kortner, a Norwegian who had jumped ship up in San Francisco, headed down to the Central Coast area, where he met the newly widowed Mrs. Peterson. A romance flourished and the two were married. Kortner eventually adopted the Peterson children.

In 1901, when Ellen was eleven years old, the Kortners, then numbering eight children, homesteaded in Tepusquet Canyon, where Mr. Kortner began to farm.

"My stepfather was a kind and quiet man. We accepted him as our father and never thought of him in any other way."

Ellen, who lived to be 103 years old, often talked of the beauty of the Tepusquet in the old days and of the beautiful sycamores growing along the creek, "before the woodpeckers killed them all."

She recalled a time when young people gathered on the bridge near their home and danced on the wooden planks to the music of Rasmus' accordion. Her brother's love for music and his playing at all of the neighborhood gatherings eventually led to his death, when his hand became infected from a blister caused by the leather of his accordion. Blood poisoning set in, and the early doctoring methods were not enough to save him.

The Kortner children attended Tepusquet School, located on the bank of the creek. Since many of her schoolmates came from old Spanish families and Spanish was spoken out on the playground, Ellen became fluent in three languages—English, Spanish and Danish.

In June of 1905 Ellen Kortner married George Robert Tunnell, and the two moved to an 80-acre parcel on the old Tunnell homestead in Santa Maria, land that he'd inherited from his father. The two remained on the property throughout their married life, farming beans and grains and raising cattle.

Before her marriage, Ellen and her sister had a little dressmaking business in which the girls would go out to various houses and spend three or four days of fitting, pinning, basting and sewing dresses for their clients. The business came to an end when Ellen married.

The Tunnells had two children, Teresa and George Curtis. Curtis Tunnell served on the Santa Maria City Council, was Mayor from 1956 to 1960, and was the 5th District's representative to the Santa Barbara County Board of Supervisors from 1963 to 1975.

George Tunnell sold his 80-acre plot of land to

Ellen Kortner Tunnell celebrated her 100th birthday in 1980 with her children, grandchildren and great-grandchildren gathered around her. At center, rear, are son Curtis and daughter Teresa; flanking them are Curtis' sons Curtis and George; and filling out the scene are Curtis and George's children, John, Mary, Katie and Anne.

Captain Hancock in January of 1926 and passed away the following June. In the fall of that year, the Tunnell house was moved from the homesteaded property into town at 129 West Tunnell Street.

In September of 1980, Ellen Kortner Tunnell celebrated her 100th birthday, with 96 of those years having been spent living in the Santa Maria Valley. An article appearing in the *Santa Maria Times* commemorating the event told of her always being active in civic affairs. She was a member of the Presbyterian Church in Santa Maria as well as the Order of Eastern Star, the Rebeccas and the Danish Ladies' Society.

Ellen Kortner Tunnell died in February of 1984 at the age of 103 and is buried in the Santa Maria Cemetery next to George Robert Tunnell, the man she had married 79 years before. 🐢

The Santa Maria Inn

VEN THOUGH all of his friends thought that he'd lost his mind when he gave up his job with Union Sugar to go into the hotel business, and businessmen felt that he was tackling the impossible, the man refused to listen.

"There comes a time when a man tires of working for others, no matter how fine the salary, so I decided to build a hotel and run it."

Frank McCoy came from a long line of industrious people. Although his two brothers, George and Hugh, were born in the United States, Frank was born in Ireland while his pregnant mother was over there settling an estate.

In 1904, McCoy, then 28 years old, arrived in the Santa Maria Valley to work for the Union Sugar Company in Betteravia, where one of his duties was to arrange for the housing and feeding of the company's employees. While doing extensive traveling in connection with his work, he discovered the almost total lack of comfortable hotel accommodations for the traveling man.

As a sideline, he leased some land, planted beans and sold them to the federal government. By 1915, when his bean venture had given him the means with which to form a business of his own, McCoy resigned from the sugar plant, took a year's vacation, and traveled up and down the coast in search of a suitable site for the hotel of his dreams.

While staying at the Bradley Hotel in Santa Maria, he became interested in the abandoned Blochman house located on the outskirts of town on South Broadway. Even though the house was almost hidden by many trees and overgrown bushes, he could visualize its possibilities.

McCoy began negotiations for the purchase of the property, which the Blochmans had left in 1909 when they moved to Berkeley. After the purchase was completed and he received title to the property, he proceeded with plans to convert the house into a hotel. Since the old English inns had impressed him during his many travels, he had Oscar Doane design the same style of building. In 1916 construction began on the first addition of what was to become the Santa Maria Inn.

Although the Blochman house site was the ideal setting for the type of hostel that McCoy wanted to build, his friends, who were sure that he'd gone mad for attempting such a venture, advised him to get rid of the jungle so that people could at least see the buildings.

McCoy kept the eucalyptus trees, which had been planted by James F. Goodwin in 1879, as well as the old magnolia and palm trees standing directly in front of the inn's entrance, and planted other trees.

As May 16, 1917, dawned bright and clear, the Santa Maria Inn opened its doors with 24 bedrooms and 24 baths, as well as a kitchen and dining room ready to serve the tastes of its most discriminating guests. As an added touch, McCoy's lifelong collection of copper, pewter, carved chests and historical documents tastefully dotted the interior.

Ray P. Cooney, district manager for National Supply Company and a long-time friend of McCoy, was the first person to register. Almost 36 years later, Cooney passed away at his friend's inn.

The people that McCoy personally selected to help him run his hotel became loyal employees and friends who remained with him for many years. Fred Pimentel, who went to work for McCoy when the Inn opened, worked his way up to the position of manager, and stayed at the Inn until shortly after McCoy's death, when he moved across the street to take over as manager of the Santa Maria Club. William Mizell Funk, who began working at the Inn in 1926, remained there until 1953, when he joined the Santa Barbara Sheriff's Department.

The Santa Maria Inn dining room

McCoy's love of flowers was evident, as fresh flowers from his private gardens filled the dining room windows and lobby, giving birth to the saying, "It's always blossom time at the Santa Maria Inn."

Contrary to his friends' earlier predictions of sure failure, McCoy's Inn was such a stunning success that it soon became necessary to add additional rooms. By 1928 the Inn had 85 rooms and was attracting the elite and well known from all over the world.

In addition to developing his Inn, McCoy was active in community affairs. Not only did he help to promote the growth of the Santa Maria Union High School while serving as clerk on the board of trustees, but he also helped several boys and girls in the community to obtain a college education.

This quiet and unobtrusive man served on the library board, was a member of the city's planning commission, and served on a committee that was set up to build a new Methodist Church. He was also instrumental in the restoration of the San Ramon Chapel near Sisquoc, and helped promote the building of Our Lady of Perpetual Help Hospital in Santa Maria.

Although McCoy became a successful man, making money wasn't his only object in life. "Follow the Golden Rule," he'd often say, "and material things will take care of themselves."

Frank McCoy passed away on December 10, 1949, at the age of 77. Two years later, at the 26th annual Pioneer Day Picnic at Waller Park, he was remembered as the one person who had contributed the most to the growth and development of the community during the first 50 years of the 20th century.

The hostelry on South Broadway stands as a monument to the man whose vision was responsible for creating the Santa Maria Inn, a building which remains a hallmark of elegance. ✥

From Portugal to Oso Flaco

HE PORTUGUESE PEOPLE who began to arrive in the Oso Flaco area from the Azores in the late 1800s brought with them expertise in dairy farming. Like the Swiss-Italians who came to the area at about the same time, they were incredibly hard workers. Those who didn't operate dairy farms grew beans, with some becoming very successful during World War I, when they contracted with the United States government to grow the beans that fed half the world. When the war ended, so did their contracts with the government.

The success of the farmers, although not bringing great wealth, did provide a comfortable living. Many Portuguese people continued to farm in the local area, with some dry farming on Oso Flaco property leased from the LeRoys of France.

Since most of the Portuguese people coming from the Azores are Catholic, many of their social events are linked to the church. One such custom has roots going back to the 13th century when Queen Isabel of Portugal, born in 1271, ruled the land.

Queen Isabel is particularly noted for having dedicated her life to the poor by establishing orphanages as well as providing the less fortunate with food and shelter.

During a great famine, the Queen made a vow to the Holy Spirit that if food arrived from England to feed her country, she would find the poorest girl in the land and make her a Queen for a day. Almost immediately, so the story goes, ships loaded with enough food to feed the hungry arrived, after which both classes shared a meal prepared by the nobility.

This act, creating a sense of equality and brotherly love, is celebrated each year throughout the Portuguese communities of the world.

Family troubles toppled the queen from the throne. When she finally regained it, she dedicated a church to the Holy Spirit as a gesture of gratitude. The royal crown, which had been placed in the sanctuary, was given back to her at a service of thanksgiving followed by a public feast.

Every year, beginning on Pentecost Sunday, the 7th Sunday after Easter, and continuing throughout the month of August, the Central Coast Portuguese communities celebrate this miracle.

The celebration begins when a queen and two princesses lead a parade of parishioners to the church, where a priest is waiting to meet them at the door. The queen presents him with her crown, which he then places on the altar. When Mass has ended, he returns the crown to the queen. The procession begins again when the queen and the parade of parishioners proceed to the parish hall to feast on *sopes,* the traditional Portuguese dish. Money earned from these festas support scholarships.

The local Portuguese social life is centered around the DES Club on Chapel Street near Depot Street. This building, constructed in 1947, was built for the annual Pentecostal celebration. With much hard work by the members, the building was fully paid for in 1965.

The Novo brothers, Angelo and Frank, came from the Azores in 1902, and ran a blacksmith shop on the south side of West Main Street at the corner of Thornburgh for many years. During the depression years, they helped the local farmers by repairing their machinery, carrying the charges on their books while awaiting better times. When the depression finally ended, the brothers wiped all of the debts from their books. Their brother, Morris, had a shop in Guadalupe.

Joseph D. Brass farmed 160 acres 2½ miles from Santa Maria on West Main Street, on the north side of the street, while John B. Brass farmed property near the sugar factory in Betteravia. His son, John H. Brass, was Postmaster in Santa Maria during the 1960s.

Santa Marians of Portuguese descent continue to make headlines. Joe Olivera, who spent many years on the Santa Maria Planning Commission, was on the city's landmark committee for 14 years. In 1993 this civic-minded disabled veteran was honored by the city as Santa Maria's Citizen of the Year.

Robin Ventura, who graduated from Righetti High School, played on the baseball team that competed in the Olympic games in Seoul, Korea. After graduating from Oklahoma State, Robin went immediately into professional baseball, playing third base for the Chicago White Sox and winning 4 Golden Glove awards. He stayed with the White Sox for 9 years before moving to the New York Mets.

The Portuguese influence in the valley is evident by such names as Sousa, Teixeira, Bello, Silva, Dutra, Coelho, Trigueiro, Simas, Ventura, Santos, Azevedo, Faria, Alvernaz, Silveira, Marciel, Pereira, Jorge, Pimental, Leal, Quaresma, Gracia, Dias, Brass, Oliveira, Novo, Freitas, Serpa, Cardoza, Bettencourt and a host of others. ❧

Setsuo and George Aratani

CENTURY HAS PASSED since many Japanese men came to the United States in search of the American dream. During the following years, fortunes were made, some of which were later lost. One man's son, in picking up the pieces, went on to become one of the country's most amazing success stories.

Setsuo Aratani was no ordinary man. Born in Hiroshima in 1885, he was put in the care of wealthy relatives at the age of two when both of his parents died.

Deciding to pursue a career in commerce, he graduated from Onomichi School of Commerce, a local trade school, in 1905. Anxious to see what the new world had to offer, he left behind his fiancée, Yoshiko Matsui, and set sail for San Francisco, but not before making a promise to return and marry her as soon as he was financially set.

Aratani stayed in San Francisco for about three years, during which time he enrolled in English classes offered by one of the Christian missions.

From San Francisco, Aratani headed south, where he found employment on a strawberry farm in El Monte. Although knowing nothing about farming, he took pains to learn the business from beginning to end. It was here that his vision of establishing an operation of his own took root.

However, harsh California Alien Land Laws that had been recently enacted severely hampered the Japanese farmers. Since only citizens could own land, and Isseis were declared ineligible for citizenship, they were prevented from buying and, in most cases, leasing land.

Still, though, they needed to support their families.

Since they weren't able to purchase land, Issei farmers such as Aratani had to use a third party, a United States citizen, to purchase land on which to farm.

During this time they worked through the newly organized Guadalupe Japanese Association to help each other and to "promote the welfare of all."

In 1952 the McCarran-Walter Act finally gave

Setsuo Aratani

76

the Isseis the right to become citizens and in 1956 the state of California repealed its Alien Land Laws.

Meanwhile, in Japan, both the Matsui and Aratani families were doubtful that Setsuo would return to Yoshiko. So much time had passed since he had left his homeland that they felt that the girl should forget about him. She married a local Japanese man and bore a son and a daughter. Her husband died when the children were toddlers.

When Aratani heard of Yoshiko's situation, he offered to marry her and to take the children in as his own. However, his family opposed such an arrangement and arranged for relatives to adopt the boy, while other relatives took care of the daughter. Yoshiko then set sail for the United States, where she and Aratani were wed.

Although Aratani was making a name for himself within the local Japanese community, his greatest achievement and joy took place when his son, George, was born in 1917.

After Aratani brought his family to Guadalupe, he experimented with the growing of all kinds of vegetables, thus pioneering the vegetable industry. On July 11, 1920, he shipped the first carload of lettuce from the valley to Texas. In 1923 he and two Iseii friends organized the Guadalupe Produce Company, Guadalupe's first packing plant. He opened a branch house in Lompoc and farmed more than 4,000 acres in the two valleys. In 1936 he organized the All Star Trading Company, importing both fertilizer and sake from Japan.

He began shipping local produce, packed with crushed ice and placed into railroadw cars, to the Midwest as well as to markets along the Atlantic seaboard. Until vacuum cooling came into existence in 1941, blowers were used to fill the loaded cars with snow ice.

A true entrepreneur, Aratani saw great potential in the shipping business and encouraged his friends, who were strictly farmers, to do the same.

Those who followed his advice became very successful.

Being a "red hot" baseball fan, the personable Aratani formed his own baseball team in 1927. The team, "ARATANI," was made up of local Portuguese, Mexican, Swiss/Italian and Japanese players, and while some of the players worked for him, others were said to have been just good local ballplayers. His team members included Virgil Alexander, Charlie Moglin, Ed Clark, Tony Montez, Charlie Draper, Fred Tsuda, Wallace Arakawa, Buck Weaver, Deane Walker and others.

In 1928, after winning championships two years in a row, Aratani took his 15-member team to Japan to compete against Japanese baseball teams. The team left San Francisco on the *Korea Maru* on August 1, 1928, and by the time it returned three months later, it had racked up twenty-five wins, one tie and four losses. Eleven-year-old George Aratani accompanied his father's team and served as its bat boy and team mascot. During this trip George met both his half-brother and half-sister.

Young George looked forward to a promising career in professional baseball. As the star shortstop of Santa Maria Union High School's baseball team, he was scouted by major league ball clubs, one of which was the Pittsburgh Pirates. In 1933, he helped the Saints capture the California Interscholastic Federation state championship.

The young man's hopes of playing professional baseball ended when he was injured in a football game on Armistice Day of 1933. After the damaged cartilage was removed from his knee, any hopes of his pursuing a career in sports were dashed.

Known as a community leader, Setsuo Aratani was a past director of the Rotary Club and served on the Board of Directors of the Santa Maria Chamber of Commerce in 1939. Prominent in all youth activities, he also supported both the American Red Cross and the Salvation Army. An avid golf player, he spent many hours at the Santa Maria Country Club.

Described by those who knew him as "one of the finest and most caring individuals that the world could ever know," Mr. Aratani ("Big Boss") made it possible for many young people to seek a college education by hiring them to work at his various companies.

In 1936, the year after Aratani's wife, Yoshiko, passed away, his family in Japan arranged a mar-

riage with Yoshiko's niece, Masuko Matsui. Shortly after their marriage, the Aratanis returned to Guadalupe, where they maintained their home on Peralta Street until Mr. Aratani was diagnosed as having tuberculosis in 1939 and was taken to a hospital in Monrovia to recover.

Although his health seemed to be improving, he contracted meningitis and was taken to the Japanese Hospital in Los Angeles, where he died on April 16, 1940.

Funeral services were held at the Veterans Memorial auditorium, with Bishop Matsukage of San Francisco, head of the Buddhist church in the United States, conducting the services. Ken Kitasako, a personal friend of the family, remembered the hundreds of floral tributes literally banking the building.

After his father's death, George Aratani, then a student at Stanford University, was called home to oversee his father's companies. Less than two years later World War II broke out. Within a few short months, all Japanese people living on the West Coast were sent to internment camps located in various parts of the country.

Because of his proficiency in the Japanese language, having studied two years at the prestigious Keio University in Japan, George served during the war as an instructor at the Japanese Language School at Camp Savage, Minnesota, a school which was later moved to Fort Snelling. Paul Kurokawa of Guadalupe was also an instructor at this school. The men who were trained at this school went on to serve the country in many different capacities, with some acting as spies for the United States. Because of their expertise in reading the language, they were able to decode and read intercepted messages found in the jungles of the South Pacific. Among the valley men who participated in this great endeavor were Tad Yamada, Shoji Aoyama, and John Kawachi.

In November of 1944, Sakaye Inouye left the

George Aratani

internment camp in Poston, Arizona, and traveled to Minneapolis where she became the bride of George Aratani.

During the period of internment, all of the Aratani properties in Guadalupe were lost, with the exception of the All Star Trading Company, which had become dormant.

When the war ended and some of the Japanese returned to their homes, they found that many changes had been made while they were gone. Others chose not to return. The Tomooka brothers, who were the first to introduce broccoli to California, stayed in Arizona, where they set up a farming operation in Glendale.

Paul Kurokawa returned to Guadalupe, where, along with his parents, he ran a fish market. He later opened Paul's Liquor, a business that he ran until retiring in 1996. His was one of the oldest liquor licenses in Santa Barbara County. The Minamis

returned to Guadalupe, where they resumed farming under the name of Security Farms.

After the war, George Aratani reactivated the trading company, renaming it American Commercial, DBA Mikasa, and began opening outlet stores on the East Coast and working his way west. Mikasa china is carried in all of the major department stores located throughout the country. Always on the lookout for new ventures, the enterprising Aratani began Kenwood Electronics in the late 1950s.

The Aratanis have donated to countless worthy causes and have raised millions of dollars for Japanese Memorials both in California and Washington, D. C.

Although George Aratani achieved great success in the business sector, he never forgot that his roots were in the Santa Maria Valley. 🪆

Harry Dorsey

EVER BEFORE AND NEVER since has Santa Maria seen the likes of Harry Dorsey, the man who brought true showmanship to town.

Harry Custer Dorsey, born on a farm in Benton County, Iowa, on May 12, 1877, was the third of seven children. At the age of 12, when a circus came to town, Harry was given a free pass as payment for watering the elephants. Life was never to be the same for the young farm boy.

Having long been unhappy with unrelenting farm work from morning until night, the boy desperately wanted to get away and do something different with his life.

When Harry turned 14, he sold his bicycle and bought a ticket to Columbus, Ohio, where his aunt and uncle lived. After arriving in the city and not knowing how to find his relatives, but knowing that they were in show business, he headed straight for the theater district, where he happened to meet his uncle on the street.

Although his aunt understood his wanting to learn about show business, she insisted that he go to school. However, since Harry was more interested in getting his foot in the door of show business than going to school, he persuaded her to let him work backstage as a general laborer, where he was paid $12 a month.

After three years of working and traveling with shows out of Columbus, Harry took the $90 that he'd saved and headed for San Francisco, arriving there during the Gay Nineties period when San Francisco was a mecca for show business-related activities, and "flickers" were creating a sensation.

Harry had no trouble in finding a job. He started working for some of the traveling shows, sometimes filling in as a minstrel.

In 1906, the year after the big San Francisco earthquake, Harry met an old friend who was looking for a partner in the newly popular one-reel motion picture business.

The two early movie entrepreneurs bought film and went into business, with *The Great Train Robbery* as their first flick. Using an old Edison-type projection camera with no take-up reel, they set up a tent as their base of operation, rented chairs, and projected pictures on a bed sheet which they carried around in a grip. With film being run off into a basket, each picture ran about 15 minutes.

From San Francisco, the two showmen moved to Northern California, where they began renting legitimate theater halls to show their flicks. With swallow-tailed coats (with gold coins used for buttons) and black silk top hats, the two young men became the epitome of big time showmen.

From California, the two entrepreneurs headed southeast to Memphis, Tennessee, where they proceeded to follow the same pattern of success. When the year ended and the two men had cleared over $40,000, they realized that the motion picture industry had an incredible future.

The partners incorporated and sold stock in their newly organized "Montgomery Amusement Company," took in another partner, and, with the three of them each investing $100,000, they were on their way to success. By 1913 they were operating theaters in Georgia, Florida, South Carolina and Ohio, purchasing vaudeville houses and legitimate theaters one by one and converting them into movie houses catering to the discriminating public.

However, their uncontrolled spending was eating away at their profits. In 1917 the business collapsed, and the corporation broke up.

Dorsey then moved to Holyoke, Massachusetts, where he purchased a theater and his new wife acted as his cashier.

In 1920, when Harry found an advertisement in one of the trade magazines announcing the sale of the Gaiety Theater on East Main Street in Santa Maria, the Dorseys packed up everything they had and moved to Santa Maria.

In addition to showing the latest movies at his new theater, Dorsey managed to bring in many Hollywood stars. Santa Marians flocked to the Gaiety to see such stars as Pola Negri, Eddie Cantor, Hoot Gibson, Gary Cooper and Will Rogers. Those stars not arriving in town by private car arrived in Guadalupe via the Southern Pacific Railway and rode the local streetcar into Santa Maria.

When Dorsey, then a widower, booked the Los Angeles contralto Ethel-May Palmer to be the guest soloist at the Gaiety Theater, a romance blossomed, and the two were married in November of 1927 at the Los Angeles Presbyterian Church. They made their home at 1010 South Broadway in Santa Maria.

On April 5, 1928, the Santa Maria Theater opened on the corner of Broadway and Church Street, with Buster Keaton starring in United Artists' *Steamboat Bill*. This Spanish-styled amusement palace with a seating capacity of 1,200 was the first all-electric theater ever built.

Dorsey spared no expense in creating a theater that was the epitome of modern design and elegance.

The theater was a smashing success as Santa Marians flocked to see Dorsey's latest flick. Shortly after opening, Dorsey brought in his brother Garfield from his farm in Iowa to help him with this new venture.

The first talkies came to the Santa Maria Theater in May of 1929, when Dorsey brought in *The Innocents of Paris*.

In 1944, Dorsey's Santa Maria Amusement Company purchased the Studio Theater at 221 East Main Street from a competitor and brought in Harry's nephew, Charlie, to help run it.

In addition to serving on the Board of Directors of the Santa Maria Savings and Loan Association, he also served on the Advisory Board of the local branch of the Bank of America. He was a member of the Santa Maria Rotary Club and served as its president in 1931.

Harry Custer Dorsey passed away on February 22, 1961, and is buried in the Santa Maria Cemetery.

Odulia Dille

OADED WITH HIGH ASPIRATIONS, but with neither money nor enough education with which to pursue them, nineteen-year-old Odulia Carranza approached Dr. Bert Coblentz one day and said that she wanted to be a doctor. After learning that she had only an 8th-grade education, he knew that no medical school in the country would accept her. To soften the blow, he suggested that she have a talk with Mrs. Lang, who at that time was operating the Lucas Sanitarium.

It was with a great deal of trepidation that the young Odulia approached Mrs. Lang. The woman stood more than six feet tall and weighed over 200 pounds, and to Odulia, she was nothing short of intimidating. However, the girl knew that she'd have to put her fears behind her if she wanted to pursue her dreams. She soon learned, though, that Mrs. Lang was a very kind and understanding woman.

After the two had finished talking, Mrs. Lang told the girl to report to work the next day and went on to say that the first item on her agenda would be to buy material and have uniforms made for her, including caps. More than fifty years later, in looking back on her long career, Odulia said, "I wasn't entitled to wear a cap. But Mrs. Lang was a great nurse, and what she taught, you learned. I don't have the book knowledge, but I have the experience. I'm not afraid to work beside any nurse."

It wasn't long before Odulia was caring for the patients, dispensing drugs and assisting in the operating room. She eventually became a surgical nurse and anesthesiologist. "We handled all kinds of cases, including injuries. I still remember the first time I was present at an amputation. I was told to hold the patient's arm while Doctors Lucas and Coblentz took it off."

The pioneer Doctor William T. Lucas, for whom the sanitarium was named, took her under his wing. Holding her high in his esteem, he was known to request her nursing services up until the time that he died.

The Lucas Sanitarium at 724 South Broadway, with space for about twelve beds, had four nurses working in pairs around the clock. Putting in twelve-hour shifts, sometimes stretching to sixteen, the girls took care of the patients, did the janitorial work and washed diapers for the babies.

The nurses lived in quarters located in back of the hospital and ate in the hospital's kitchen. When Odulia's sister, Ynez, came in as a nurse trainee, the two shared a room.

During the 1918 Spanish flu epidemic, the town's physicians converted the Princess Hall on Pine Street into an infirmary. Every available person, both trained and untrained, was recruited to help with the nursing. While Odulia and the other nurses seemed to be working around the clock, with little time for sleeping, their pay remained at less than $50 a month.

In April of 1918, Odulia was the nurse in attendance when Lloyd Dille was born, never dreaming that the day would come when she'd be raising the infant that she was then holding in her arms.

One day in 1921, when Fremont "Monte"

Dille came to the sanitarium to visit his sister, who was a patient there, the two met again and a romance blossomed. By that time Monte was employed in the Taft oil fields and was separated from his wife.

Odulia, one of eight children born to Rose (Ontiveros) and Feliz Carranza, was born in Mendoza Canyon and was a great-granddaughter of Juan Pacífico and Martina (Osuna) Ontiveros. When the Carranza children were of school age, the family moved to Miguel Canyon, near Sisquoc. Rose Carranza passed away in 1901, leaving eight children ranging in age from one to fourteen.

After Odulia and Monte were married in 1923, they moved to Long Beach, where Monte found work in the booming oil fields. However, since Odulia had never been away from Santa Maria before, she cried every day. A year later the couple left the southland and came back home.

In October of the same year, Odulia was admitted in the Lucas Sanitarium, and with Doctor M. Thorner as the attending physician, she became the second woman in the area to give birth by caesarian section. Sadly, the baby, Harold Lee Dille, died in December of the same year.

Before her marriage, Odulia had switched to special duty nursing, always harboring a desire to obtain formal nurse's training. Even though Doctors Lucas, Coblentz and Thorner tried to help, a law had been passed requiring a student nurse to first have a high school diploma. Since she couldn't qualify, the doctors promised to keep her busy, and they did.

As the years passed, so did the lives of the Dille family. Monte went to work for the County of Santa Barbara, where he became superintendent of the road department and finally retired after thirty-two years of service.

According to a newspaper interview with Odulia, Mrs. Lang closed the Lucas Sanitarium and started the Lang Sanitarium. Running the sanitarium with Mrs. Lang was Jessie Grigsby, who had also worked at the Lucas hospital.

Odulia worked at the second hospital as a special duty nurse, along with notables Mary Paulding, Ione Haslam, and Rowena Marriott.

Before Mrs. Lang passed away in 1932 at the age of 62, a third private hospital, the Cottage Hospital, was operating at the corner of Vine and Church Streets, run by a Mrs. Reel. Mrs. Grigsby closed the Lang Sanitarium about that time and purchased Mrs. Reel's property at 303 East Church Street, changing the name to Grigsby Hospital. She eventually opened another hospital in Arroyo Grande.

Tragedy struck the Dille family in 1949 when Lloyd passed away. Odulia, the woman who helped to bring him into the world and later raised him, was also at his side when he died. Lloyd's widow, Frances Silva Dille, later married Joseph Trigueiro and moved with her family to Mountain Home, Arkansas.

Long after Odulia officially retired from nursing, she was still on call. When friends and relatives required her services, she was there to do the work that she did best. "I love nursing. I liked my patients and enjoyed having them recover. The doctors were wonderful and I loved them all. They were good to me and to their patients. It was different then. We did what we had to do. The doctors made house calls and knew all about the patients. Now it's cut 'em up, get 'em up and send 'em out."

In looking back on her life at the age of 82, she was asked if she'd like to live those years over again. Her predictable reply was, "I'd try harder to get an education and become a surgeon."

Monte Dille passed away in 1982 and Odulia passed away in 1990. Both are buried in the Santa Maria Cemetery. ❧

The Pioneer Association

HE IDEA OF CREATING an association of pioneers was born in 1923 when W. C. Oakley, J. A. Oakley and their nephew B. W. Stowell killed a steer and invited their pioneer friends to join them for a barbecue on the Alamo Creek.

Everyone had such a good time reminiscing about the early days of Santa Maria that one of the men suggested that the barbecue become an annual event.

When a group of early pioneers met at the Bradley Hotel on the following 14th of July, with Dr. W. T. Lucas acting as temporary chairman and C. W. Smith as secretary, the "Old Timers of Santa Maria" was organized.

F. C. Twitchell was later elected permanent chairman of the organization, with Harry Saulsbury as secretary. W. H. Rice, William Tunnell and C. W. Smith were all appointed to the executive board.

During this meeting, it was moved and carried that anyone who had come to this valley prior to 1890 should be eligible for membership, with the "valley" consisting of Sisquoc, Garey, Casmalia, Guadalupe and Santa Maria.

The group decided that the organization would not assess dues at first and that a reunion of fellow pioneers would be held at least once a year.

Since people were called on to give their first impressions of the valley, tales were told of both happy and sad times and of the wild animals, geese, horses, and the Indians. As each person related his story, dates were recorded, showing William Tunnell coming in 1868; W. C. Adam and W. C. Oakley coming in 1869; C. W. Smith in 1871; S. T. Coiner, W. H. Rice, and W. J. Brown in 1873; Harry Saulsbury in 1877; F. C. Twitchell and Judge S.E. Crow in 1878; Dr. Lucas in 1879; James Lertora in 1880, and A. L. Ames in 1883.

Within seventy years the "Santa Maria Pioneer Association," as it later became known, grew from a few members to more than a thousand.

At first the membership requirements were vague, and anyone who wanted to attend the annual barbecues merely showed up. However, in 1979, a membership drive was started, and the bylaws were changed to permit as members only those people whose ancestors arrived before 1940 and all of their descendants. People who have lived here 30 years have since been permitted to become Associate Members. To date, the Pioneer Association has almost 2,000 card-carrying members.

Since tradition dictates that the annual Santa Maria High School reunion be held on the night before the Pioneer Picnic, people participate in a double celebration.

For many years, when the Pioneer Picnic was held on the 1st of May of every year, the day was cause for a town celebration. Businesses closed for the day, and the *Santa Maria Daily Times* was filled with stories of early days of the town. Greetings and congratulations filled page after page as the town's merchants extended their good wishes to the pioneer families.

Although no official records were kept about the early days of the barbecue, Pauline Novo, who

Pioneer Santa Marians posed for a group portrait at the annual picnic on May 2, 1959.

took a personal interest in the preservation of these historic events, became the unofficial Pioneer historian and kept scrapbooks of recorded memories of each barbecue held since 1979.

The Pioneer Association annual barbecue has been held at different locations throughout the years, with the water of the Twitchell Dam now covering the site of the original barbecues. Pauline Novo remembered the annual 20-mile trip to the Cuyama with her mother. Later barbecues were held at the Union Oil Picnic Grounds up on Newlove Hill. Finally, on the 13th of July, 1996, the association's new Pioneer Park, located on the corner of Blosser Road and West Foster Road, was dedicated during the 72nd Annual Pioneer Picnic. This new park had been built with the help of volunteers and through the donations of interested friends.

On July 14, 2001, over 1000 members of the Pioneer Association and their guests met at Pioneer Park to celebrate the group's 77th Pioneer Picnic. During the festivities the Albert Novo and Pauline Lownes Novo Pavilion was dedicated in honor of the couple's hard work and dedication to the success of both the park and the association. Benches installed by Jim and Fred Carr were dedicated to the memory of their mother, Betty Haslam Carr, who had passed away earlier that year. In the back of the park, a separate area was dedicated as the "Donati Hideaway" to give honor to Clarence Donati, who chaired the group that built the Pioneer Park in 1996.

Santa Maria is one of the few communities in the state that stages an annual Pioneer Day. The town is unique in that it has been converted into a veritable paradise as a result of the foresight, determination and optimism of its original settlers. Santa Maria both honors its pioneers and venerates them. It feels a constant debt of gratitude to its ancestors who made possible the comforts and conveniences now the blessing of every Santa Marian.

Dave Boyd

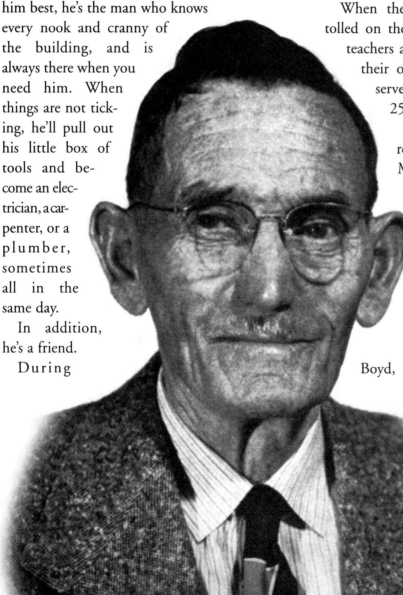

HE CUSTODIAN OF A SCHOOL, by definition, is one who is the guardian or caretaker of the building. However, for the teachers and students who know him best, he's the man who knows every nook and cranny of the building, and is always there when you need him. When things are not ticking, he'll pull out his little box of tools and become an electrician, a carpenter, or a plumber, sometimes all in the same day.

In addition, he's a friend.

During the early days of Santa Maria High School, keeping the building smoothly running was one man's personal responsibility, and his dedication knew no bounds. In addition to always being on call, the custodian was loved and respected by everyone.

When the Santa Maria High School's bell tolled on the morning of December 17, 1929, teachers and students instinctively knew that their own Jim "Dad" Murphy, who had served as the school's custodian for over 25 years, was gone.

Appointed in 1902 through the recommendation of L. E. Blochman, Murphy had served the school until 1928, when his age and failing strength made it necessary for him to retire. Even though Mr. Murphy was officially retired, he returned to the school every day to ring the morning bell, and continued to do so until the day that death claimed him.

After Mr. Murphy retired, David Boyd, who had served the school since 1922, took his place. Boyd, who had left Ireland when he was four years old, worked in a variety of jobs before he found Santa Maria.

While attending college in San Jose, Boyd was drafted into the Army and served in the Spanish-

American War. The variety of jobs that he held in his lifetime prepared him for the jack-of-all-trades position of custodian. He had driven a stage, served as master man on a streetcar, worked for Southern Pacific Railroad, served as warehouse foreman at Southern Pacific Milling, and had worked at the shipyards during World War I. He had even worked in the oil fields.

He was helping to build the Orcutt School at the time that the high school was being built. However, on November 1, 1922, when he was offered the job of serving under Mr. Murphy, he left the Orcutt job and reported to Murphy, ready to go to work.

After his appointment as the school custodian, he lived in a house once located on the site of the present football field. He is remembered as being a man who devoted his time and efforts to the well-being of the school and seemed to be able to fix anything.

Dave Boyd loved to dance, and had even run a dancing school in Hollister for three years. Whenever music started to play, whether it was a waltz or a polka, he and his wife, Carrie, were the first out on the dance floor. "I never miss a week going dancing someplace," Dave once said.

According to Jim May, Dave Boyd made it his personal responsibility to see that everything was done right, whether it was preparing for the school play or controlling lights for the various sporting events held at the school. In 1959 he had 10 custodians and gardeners working for him.

George Hobbs, who worked for Mr. Boyd while attending junior college, echoed the sentiments of those who remembered the man as being "just a well-respected, nice guy."

When the word went out to "call Dave," everyone could rest assured that Mr. Boyd would be there in a flash, dressed in his bib overalls, ready to get things running again.

As an active member of the community, Boyd served as president of the Pioneer Association, was a member of the Santa Maria Valley Historical Society, and was a member of the Order of Red Men.

When Dave Boyd died in December of 1963 and was buried at the Santa Maria Cemetery, a military service, honoring his service during the Spanish-American War, was held at the gravesite.

The high school's football field is named the "David Boyd Athletic Field" in recognition of the man's long devoted service to the school. 🕱

Louis Noire Crawford

ouis Noire Crawford, the renowned valley architect, was born May 31, 1890, on a farm in Louisville, Kentucky. Upon completion of his high school education, he spent two years studying civil engineering at Purdue University. After teaching for four years, he enrolled in the Illinois University,

where he earned his B. S. degree in engineering. Upon completion of additional course work in both Michigan and California universities, he became certified to practice architecture in the states of Illinois and California.

In 1915 Crawford took a position with the University of California during its summer session. While teaching in Berkeley, he met Winifred Kittredge, whom he married in December of 1917. Three years later he joined the faculty of Santa Maria High School, where he introduced and coached (with "Cap" Twitchell serving as captain) the first team of modern football. He also coached the American Legion football team for three years.

When Mr. Crawford opened his private practice as architect here in 1920, it marked the beginning of a career that earned him a reputation as the designer of Santa Maria's "most beautiful buildings."

In addition to Mr. Crawford's designing the Santa Maria Gas Company annex and the Knights of Pythias buildings, his expertise can be seen in many of the area's schools. Some of the schools that were constructed under his direction included Orcutt, El Camino, Fairlawn, Goleta, Vista del Mar, Arroyo Grande, Pismo Beach, Cayucos, and Morro Bay elementary schools. Other schools included San Luis Obispo High School and Junior High School, plus the Cambria Pines high school buildings.

In May of 1983, a plaque was placed and dedicated by Mayor George Hobbs in Santa Maria's City Hall honoring Mr. Crawford as having been the man who, along with Francis Parsons, designed the city's administrative building almost fifty years before.

The building's Spanish design was influenced by Parsons' trip to Spain, Italy, France and North Africa, where he took many pictures of buildings of similar design. It's generally felt that the Spanish motif, with its tiled Moorish tower, embodies the spirit of early California mission style of architecture.

Construction of Santa Maria's City Hall was completed by the Public Works Administration in 1934 at a cost of $63,000, and was dedicated in September of that same year. The building's furniture was designed and custom-built by Gaylord Jones, a Santa Maria decorative craftsman. Mayor Marion Rice presided over the first City Council meeting held in the new building the following month. Council members present at that time included Albert Dudley, Alfred Roemer, Merle Willits, and Charles Bates.

During its early days, City Hall housed the City Judge, the Chamber of Commerce and the California Department of Motor Vehicles. The city's jail once occupied the second floor.

In 1935, when the population of Santa Maria reached 5000, the second home of the Santa Maria Elks Lodge No. 1538, located at the corner of East Main and Vine Streets, was designed by the organization's Past Exalted Ruler, Louis Noire Crawford.

In 1939, when Mr. Crawford suffered his first stroke, he was serving as Vice-President of the

Crawford's masterpiece: Santa Maria City Hall

Association of California Architects, for which he was also a district adviser. He was also a member and Past President of the American Institute of Architects and of the Santa Barbara chapter of Alpha Rho Chi architectural fraternity.

In 1940, Mr. Crawford took in Phillip J. Daniel as a partner, and the firm of Crawford and Daniel designed the city's library and the south wing of the Santa Maria High School building.

Since many of the schools designed by Mr. Crawford were built before the stringent earthquake act went into effect, many of his buildings had to be torn down. However, many others were retrofitted.

The Lucia Del Mar school has since become a historical landmark, as has been Santa Maria's City Hall.

Mr. Crawford also designed many private residences in the area, such as the DeMartin house at 115 East Camino Colegio.

In addition to his being an active member of the Masonic and B.P.O.E. lodges, Mr. Crawford was also a past president of the Santa Maria Rotary Club.

In July of 1946, Louis N. Crawford suffered a second stroke and passed away at a local hospital, leaving his widow, Winifred, and two daughters, Marjorie Crawford Martin of Santa Maria and Dorothy Crawford Hussey of Seattle, Washington. Winifred Crawford passed away in 1968 and is buried next to her husband in the Santa Maria Cemetery. 🌿

The Stewart Family

LTHOUGH HE SERVED an apprenticeship with an expert shoemaker while still a young boy, he wasn't ready to pursue this trade. Life had many adventures in store for the young man from West Virginia.

William Stewart, who had come to California in the spring of 1860 and later settled in the little town of Cambria, went to work in a general store as a clerk and accountant for several years before moving to the town of Morro, where he opened a general store.

A few years later, Stewart and his wife, Cora Jessie (Ivins), moved to San Luis Obispo, where William worked as cashier with the original Bank of San Luis Obispo, a position that he held for thirteen years. From San Luis Obispo, the couple, along with sons William and Raymond Allynne, moved to a 2500-acre cattle ranch in Klamath County, Oregon. The length of time that they spent in the Pacific Northwest is unclear, as during that time they were said to have lived for a time in Hawaii.

His decision to sell his property in Oregon and move to Santa Paula, California, to open a family shoe store marked the beginning of a business that flourished for almost 50 years.

In 1907 the Stewart family moved to Santa Maria, where William and his two sons formed a partnership and opened the town's first shoe store, the Stewart Brothers Shoe Store and Wardrobe, at 104 West Main Street. The store catered to the needs of the local people in selling shoes as well as

other leather goods.

When William passed away in 1916 at the age of 76, the store became the property of his two sons, Raymond Allynne and William.

While visiting his grandparents in Glendale, Ray met Mary Corazza. After the two were married in 1922, they made their home in Santa Maria, where their two sons, Robert Ralph and Jack Edward, were born.

Ray and Bill, with Mary helping out, ran the shoe store until the business was sold in 1945. Ray later worked as manager of the Elk's Club (where he had served as Exalted Ruler during the years 1932/33), and then out at the sugar factory in Betteravia. He passed away in 1967 at the age of 83.

Robert Ralph Stewart, one of Raymond's two sons, lived in Guadalupe for many years, where he ran a wholesale dairy business, delivering milk and dairy products to homes and stores.

During that time he also served as Justice Court Judge, a position to which he was elected seven times. While serving in that capacity, he performed the ceremony that united his brother, Jack Edward, and Nancy Alsing in matrimony.

When the position title was changed from Justice Court Judge to Municipal Court Judge, and a law degree became a requirement for the position, Stewart stepped down. He had the distinction in being one of the last laymen judges to serve in California.

Bob's wife, Annette (Mahoney) Stewart, was a prominent educator in both Guadalupe and Santa Barbara. Their son, Robert Patrick Stewart, continued in his father's footsteps and became owner of the local Knudsen distributorship.

After World War II, when Jack Edward was discharged from the Merchant Marines and Bob was discharged from the Army Air Corps, the two returned to Guadalupe, where they began repairing and selling cars. Jack Edward later went to work for W. B. Johnson Chevrolet (later to become Home Motors). After working there for about fifteen years, he opened his own car lot, a dealership that evolved into Stewart Olds-Honda-Yamaha in Santa Maria.

After Jack Stewart passed away in 1988, his wife Nancy and two sons Barry and Jeff ran the auto dealership.

Barry Stewart, following his grandfather's footsteps, served as Exalted Ruler of the Santa Maria B.P.O.E. #1538 during 1998/99.

A curious twist to the history of the Stewart family took place when the Donovan Farm was sold and a two-story house, which had been rented out to farm workers, was about to be torn down.

When Van Diaz, a Santa Maria policeman, asked for the chimney's bricks, bricks that had been made by the local Gamble Brick Yard, he was given permission to take them as long as he dismantled the chimney himself. While removing the bricks from the chimney, he found a lady's high-buttoned shoe with the inside label reading: "Stewart Brothers Shoe Company of Santa Maria, California"—the company once owned by Ray and Bill Stewart.

When Diaz approached one of the Stewart family members, the man was astonished that a relic from his ancestors would still exist. Naturally, he wanted it, but Diaz wasn't ready to part with his newfound treasure, at least not at that time. "When I'm ready to part with the shoe, I'll give it to the family," he said. 🐚

Ray and Mary Stewart

Morris Stephan

I N December of 1912, when Paul and Ida Stephan brought their two children from their comfortable home in Los Angeles to a barren sandy 60-acre plot of land located four miles south of Santa Maria, the road from Orcutt to Santa Maria was only partially surfaced. Although a few automobiles could be seen on the road, people mostly traveled in buggies or wagons.

Both Frances and Morris Stephan were born in the Los Angeles area, but because 6-year-old Morris was a sickly child, the family doctor advised his parents to take the boy to "open air."

Upon arrival in the valley, where there was nothing but open air, Paul and h i s father began to build a shed made of pine and redwood to provide a temporary shelter for the family. With no electricity, gas or water, the family had to make do with coal oil lamps and lanterns while meals were cooked on a wood stove.

The Stephan family lived in the shed for several months while Paul and his father built a more permanent four-room house for the family. With water hauled into the house in barrels, every drop was precious. With the ever-present danger of contamination in water stored in barrels, the water had to be boiled on the wood stove.

After Paul was successful in finding water on the property, he installed a gasoline generated pump and shared his water with other people who were moving into the area until they were able to dig wells and produce their own water.

As a protection from the heavy westerly winds, Paul planted some blue-gum trees west of the house. He later planted fruit trees and berries.

Twice a week Mrs. Stephan harnessed up the horse and buggy and drove to Santa Maria with her butter, eggs, fruit and vegetables. The money she earned from her sales in town paid for the bare necessities of life.

Both Frances and Morris attended eight years of elementary school at the one-room district school, George Washington. Morris' first teacher, Frances Tilley, rode a horse and buggy to school from Santa Maria.

The Stephan children attended the two-story Santa Maria Union High School, where Morris played on the legendary football team of 1923. The Saints, coached by Hugh Welch, had

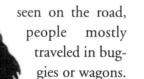

Photo courtesy of the Stephan family and Rod Rodenberger

scored an average of 60 points each game up to the semi-finals played at Long Beach.

Morris became both class president and student body president in 1924 and graduated in June of that same year.

After graduating from high school, Morris entered Santa Maria Junior College, where he again became student body president and helped to organize the school's first football team. He transferred to USC as a sophomore, and after receiving his BA degree, continued his studies at the USC School of Law, graduating in June of 1930. In September of that same year, after passing the bar examination, he took a position with the law firm of Preisker, Goble, and Twitchell.

In 1931 Morris J. Stephan married Lois Rice, and the two built their home at 920 South McClelland Street in 1939.

In 1942 he enlisted in the Naval Air Force, where he served as legal officer and civilian personnel officer as well as on the courts-martial board. After being discharged in 1946 with the rank of Lieutenant Commander, Morris came home and became a partner in the law office of Preisker, Goble, Twitchell and Stephan.

In 1948 he acquired an interest in the Ford Motor Company agency, then owned by Bowers and Stokes in Santa Maria. He sold this interest in 1950, the year before he was elected Judge of the Justice Court.

In 1950 Stephan ran for the office of Justice of the Peace of the 7th Judicial District in Santa Maria, was elected and took office in January of the following year. With the population greatly increasing with the growth of Vandenberg Air Force Base, court cases mushroomed. Stephan was re-elected and served his terms until, by a decree of the Superior Court in 1961, the Justice Court became the Municipal Court.

Morris Stephan was later appointed by the Governor as Judge of the Superior Court of Santa Barbara County. When he retired from the bench in 1972, he had been serving in judicial offices for twenty-two years. Although the man was officially retired, he often returned to the courthouse to officiate at weddings.

Both Morris and Lois Stephan were active in the First Christian Church in Santa Maria, with Morris serving as Deacon.

In 1986 the Stephans moved to San Jose in order to be closer to their three children, who were then living in the Bay area.

In 1988 Morris J. Stephan passed away in San Jose; he is buried in the Santa Maria Cemetery.

Porter Clevenger

ORTER CLEVENGER, son of Steve and Edith May (Finney) Clevenger, was born in Arroyo Grande in May of 1890. After graduating from high school in Arroyo Grande in 1909, he moved to Orcutt, where he worked in the oil fields, a career that lasted until after World War II. Although he went to Los Angeles in 1911 and worked in the La Brea fields for two years, he returned to Orcutt in 1913, working as a gauger for the La Graciosa and the Pinal Dome Company, which was taken over by the Union Oil Company in 1915.

His father, Steve Clevenger, a newspaperman all of his life, had been one of the founders and the managing editor of the *Santa Maria Times*. The elder Mr. Clevenger lived in Santa Maria until 1888, when he moved to Arroyo Grande and started the *Arroyo Grande Herald,* later the *Times Press Recorder.* He passed away in Arroyo Grande in 1910.

Porter's mother worked with her husband as a general reporter, was prominent in community affairs and served as clerk of the high school board at Arroyo Grande for many years. After his father passed away, Porter helped his mother run the newspaper for about a year until she took sick and the newspaper was sold. She passed away in Los Angeles in 1912.

In February of 1910, Porter Clevenger married Cora A. Bennett, daughter of Frank E. Bennett, who served as mayor of Arroyo Grande for many years, and who also ran a local grocery store. Cora's maternal grandfather was a Civil War veteran, having served on the Union side. The Clevengers had five children.

Always interested in education, Porter Clevenger began serving as trustee on the Santa Maria High School Board in 1923. He was a member of the Masons, the Hesperian Lodge of Santa Maria (of which he was Past Master), and was a member of Newlove Camp of the Woodmen of

Porter Clevenger's graduation picture, Arroyo Grande High School, 1909

the World. With a lifetime interest in scouting, he served as chairman of the troop committee for Troop #1 of the Orcutt chapter of the Boy Scouts of America.

Porter Clevenger is remembered for dearly loving all types of sports. During his lifetime he played in just about every sport that was available. When his oldest daughter, June, was born, he was playing on a minor league baseball team. He played shortstop as well as pitcher for the Union Oil baseball team, and also participated in a soccer league in the 1930s. He was also an avid camper and fisherman. His daughter-in-law, Barbara Clevenger, remembered him breaking his leg playing football when he was 35 years old. When his advancing age prevented him from playing contact sports, Port took up bowling, in addition to fishing and camping.

According to Kathleen Thayer, her grandfather was a family man, loved to tell stories, had a great sense of humor, and was lots of fun to be with. His 13 grandchildren loved him dearly.

About fifteen years after Mr. Clevenger retired from the Oil Company, he was the proud Grand Marshall of the Orcutt Christmas Parade.

After suffering a stroke, Mr. Clevenger passed away in 1972 and is buried in the Santa Maria Cemetery. 🏵

Filipinos Come to Santa Maria

N OCTOBER 18, 1587, fifty years before the first English settlement of Jamestown was established, the Spanish galleon *Nuestra Señora de Esperanza* arrived in Morro Bay. The landing party, which included some Filipino seamen, took possession of the area in the name of Spain, using a ritual of putting up a cross made of branches. On the second day, when Indians attacked the group on shore, the men retreated to the ship, but not before one of the Filipinos had been killed.

In 1763, what is called the first wave of Filipinos to North America made its permanent settlement in the bayous of Louisiana, when sailors and navigators on board Spanish galleons jumped ship to escape the brutality of their Spanish masters.

In 1781, Antonio Miranda Rodríguez Poblador, a Filipino, was one of 45 people sent by the Spanish government to establish what is now known as the city of Los Angeles.

After the Spanish-American War, the Philippines ended its connection with Spain, and through the Treaty of Paris (April 11, 1899), Spain sold the Philippines to the United States for $20 million, thus ending over 300 years of Spanish colonization of the islands.

The second wave of Filipinos—and the first wave to California—took place between 1906 and 1934, when plantation owners went to the Philippines to recruit workers for their plantations in Hawaii.

The Immigration Act of 1924, ending the Gentlemen's Agreement of 1907, closed the doors to Japanese immigration to the United States, thereby depriving West Coast farmers of workers. The agriculture industry on the West Coast, in feeling the void of workers, began to bring in young, single Filipinos to work in their fields.

Although the Philippine islands was a territory of the United States, Filipinos could neither vote nor own land or businesses in America until after World War II. California laws were even more stringent, and laws were passed forbidding interracial marriages. With few Filipino women living in the United States, some of the men intermarried with other nationalities, but were forced to leave the state in order to do so. They later returned with their new wives.

When the migrant workers of the early '30s followed the crops throughout California, many came to Guadalupe and Santa Maria, where the single men who were able to find jobs and were not doing contract work lived in farm

Santiago Salutan (lower left) and Mac Cabaong (lower right) with their co-workers, taken 1932 near Surf, Calif. Mr. Salutan later worked for Fred Donati, Point Sal Farm, Guadalupe, 1948-1980.

96

labor camps provided by the growers. Those with families who wanted their children to have stability and a good education worked the land, sometimes for $1 a day. Those who didn't live in small houses located on the property lived in town. After one of the labor camp houses burned down in 1969 and two

Cpl. Jose Castanares (top right), 1st Filipino Infantry, Fort Ord, Calif. 25 July 1942.

people died, the county filed suit for condemnation and tore them all down.

When World War II broke out in 1941 and two Filipino Infantry regiments were formed to help liberate the Philippines—one at Camp Cooke and one in San Luis Obispo—among many who enlisted from the valley were Arthur Campaomor, Frank Paduganan, Ray Abella, Nemeshio Juanich, and Ted LaBastida.

Some of those who left the valley to enlist in the Navy included Henry Abadajos and his brother "Bully," Felix Oliva and Benny Curaza. Cardy Oliva served with the Merchant Marines. After the war, many of the members of the Filipino regiments returned to live in the valley, with some bringing war brides with them.

Another wave of Filipino immigration came in 1946 when 60,000 Filipinos who fought with the United States forces in World War II were allowed to come to live in America.

During the Great Depression, most Filipinos living in the area shared with each other rather than accept charity. They were hard working and civic-minded people who, during the war, heavily participated in every War Bond drive in the valley.

By the 1970s the more educated Filipinos came.

In 1994 Filipino veterans of World War II were finally granted United States citizenship, and approximately 26,000 Filipino veterans are now living in the United States.

It has been said that the early Filipino pioneers, in overcoming hardships and discrimination, smoothed the path for the newcomers. They helped create unions up and down the West Coast, with some of them working as organizers long before the United Farm Workers began their organizing campaigns.

Many Filipinos made their mark in the Santa Maria Valley. Connie Abella, who came in the late 1930s, was a noted fashion designer. Ted La Bastida, a prominent member of the local Filipino community, came to the Santa Maria Valley in 1928 and operated a farm off of Blosser Road. The FCBA market, run by Geronimo Arca, served the people in Guadalupe for many years. Filipinos have also held prominent positions within the local government.

From the time that these first immigrants arrived in the valley, Filipinos worked hard to support their families and to encourage them to strive for higher education. Today, those children are included in the list of Santa Maria's doctors, engineers, accountants, educators and other professionals.

With no exception, those immigrants, in wanting their children to have a better life than they did, stressed both education and responsibility for their fellow man.

On October 21, 1995, the Central Coast Chapter (Santa Maria) of the Filipino American National Historical Society dedicated a historical marker near the site in Morro Bay where the Filipinos first set foot in 1587. Choi Slo, the Chumash Indian who gave the meaningful prayer ceremony, proudly mentioned that his father was Filipino. 🏵

The Nicolai Family

IKE MANY OTHER SWISS/ Italians, Alfredo and Delfinia (Tomasini) Nicolai left their homeland and came to this area from the Canton Ticino because of stories that had filtered back to them about the Santa Maria Valley's wonderful mild climate and year-round growing seasons, much the same as those of their homeland.

Shortly after the couple arrived in the valley in 1892, Alfredo bought 25 acres of land in the area now known as West Betteravia Road for $10 in gold and began to do some dry farming. In the late 1890s, when the narrow gauge railroad cut through the Nicolai property on its way out to Betteravia, the family gave it a right of way. That right of way later became part of Betteravia Road.

When Alfredo died in the early 1900s, leaving his widow to support five children, it was a prelude of hard times yet to come. Additional tragedy struck in 1914 when Delfinia passed away, leaving four sons and a daughter to fend for themselves.

With Olympia, then about 14 years old, assuming the role of mother, the five children lived alone on the property, where they continued to farm the land and do their level best to survive.

The Nicolais remained isolated. Even though most people in Santa Maria were hardly aware of their existence, the children made periodic trips into town to sell eggs and milk in order to put food on their table. Those everyday struggles for the barest forms of survival left indelible marks on their minds as they learned, by absolute necessity, the value of the dollar.

Life became easier when oil was discovered on the Nicolai property in the 1930s, but the family's lifestyle never changed.

After Olympia married Joe Matasci, a cattle rancher from Lompoc, she went to live with him on his ranch. The couple had one adopted daughter, Virginia.

Joining other patriotic farmers in the area, the Nicolais deeded three acres of property to the federal government for a paltry sum of $100 during World War II for its use in building the Santa Maria Air Base. Later, when the federal government gave that same property to the Airport District, the family's hopes of ever regaining those few acres were dashed.

Although the family agreed that the final rights of ownership to the remaining land would go to the last surviving family member, the agreement was altered when Albert married. Wanting to have property separate from his family, he gave up his rights to the property and, in return, was deeded a half-acre of land on which to build a house at the corner of Betteravia and "A" Street in 1938. He later deeded the house to his brother, Frank, who was working on his sister's ranch in Lompoc. Frank eventually sold the house to his brother, Alfred.

Alfred lived in the original Nicolai residence, with his wife, Katherine, until 1939, when he built a house at 841 E. Cypress Street, where their daughter, Sandra, was raised.

Even after moving to the property on Cypress and renting out the old family house on Betteravia, Alfred continued to go out to the property every weekend to take care of its many fruit trees.

Like his brothers, Alfred was not a very tall man and, although he seldom spoke of his family's earlier poverty and hardships, the memories dominated his life. His wife, Katherine, was liked and respected as a private duty nurse at Sisters' Hospital for many years.

The Nicolai boys, who kept pretty much to themselves, seldom talked about their lives. Although Olympia tended to be more talkative, no one thought about asking her questions until after she had died. Stephen, the oldest, died shortly after World War II. The Nicolais weren't noted for socializing; although Alfred was a Mason, he rarely attended the organization's meetings. However, he took great pride when the organization presented him with a 50-year pin. He graduated from Santa Maria Junior College, where he majored in Business, and went to work at the Southern Pacific Milling Company. He later worked in inventory control for the Santa Maria Valley Railroad.

The original old family home, located on the north end of the property, remained vacant for a long period of time and was finally destroyed in the late 1980s after having suffered extensive damage from vandalism.

When seven acres of land were sold to a developer in 1994, Albert's old house on the corner of Betteravia and "A" Street was donated to the Boy Scouts of America and was moved next door to the Regency Hotel on Skyway Drive. With some improvements, the house continues to serve as the area headquarters for the Boys Scouts.

Sandra, daughter of Alfred and Katherine, married Richard Chenoweth. The couple had three sons—Steven, Jeff and Jason—all three of whom lived for a time at the house on the old family property. The 25 acres of land purchased by Alfredo and Delfinia Nicolai in 1892 for $10 are now part

of various housing developments and would scarcely be recognized as having once been a means of the only support of five orphaned children.

Katherine Nicolai passed away in 1976, a loss from which her husband never recovered. Alfred, the last of the five Nicolai children, passed away in 1994 at the age of 91. ❧

Katherine and Alfred Nicolai

The Southern Cross

AFTER CHARLES LINDBERGH became a national hero with his historic 1927 solo flight across the Atlantic Ocean from Long Island to Paris, people were raring to get off the ground and fly up into the air.

New airlines were springing up throughout the country, and although they were unable to offer trips matching the distance of Lindbergh's historic flight, they managed to match his discomfort. In an attempt to muffle the roaring sounds of the engines, passengers stuffed cotton wool into their ears, and the higher the plane flew, the colder the inside of the cabin became.

While Lindbergh's flight was capturing the imagination of millions, two young pilots in Australia joined forces to make a 7,500-mile flight around Australia. Captain Charles Kingsford-Smith, an Australian and former World War I flying ace, and his friend and co-pilot, Charles Ulm of San Francisco, both fostered the ambition of one day completing the same type of flight as Lindbergh. However, instead of flying across the Atlantic Ocean, their flight would originate in California and cross the Pacific Ocean to Australia in Smithy's rebuilt trimotor plane, the *Southern Cross,* a Fokker F7 high-wing monoplane powered by three Wright Whirlwind engines.

Smithy, though, was unable to get the necessary financing, as his ambitions were viewed as being difficult, risky and useless. Too many pilots had already perished while attempting such an adventure.

With his debts seemingly insurmountable and the *Southern Cross* going on the auction block because of unpaid bills, Smithy was in despair.

About this time, he was introduced to the wealthy industrialist Captain G. Allan Hancock, a man who was soon to open one of America's first schools for pilots at Santa Maria's Hancock Field. A short time later, Smithy and Ulm joined Hancock on a cruise to Mexico aboard Hancock's boat, *Oaxaca.* After 10 days at sea, Hancock asked the aviators what their plans were and how much money was needed. He offered to buy the plane, which would allow the men to pay off their debts and use the plane for their proposed flight.

*Charles Ulm and Captain
Charles Kingsford-Smith*

Captain Allan Hancock with the Southern Cross, *1928*

"You are going to fly to Australia in the *Southern Cross,*" he told them. "I don't know just how yet, but we will take the matter up later. Rest assured, however, that you are going."

Hancock had the plane overhauled and persuaded the aviators to add an experienced navigator and radioman to their crew.

On May 25, 1928, with Smithy and Ulm in the cockpit, Harry Lyon serving as navigator and Jim Warner as radioman, the *Southern Cross* was flown from Santa Monica to Santa Maria. The plane left the Santa Maria Airfield for Oakland where, in the early morning hours of May 31, the bright blue plane, loaded with fuel and supplies, was taxied out to the dirt runway, ready to begin

its historic flight. At 8:45 a.m., silence fell over the crowd gathered at the airport as Smithy gave the signal to remove the wheel chocks. The 220 HP engines roared into action and the big plane lumbered across the field, its tires bulging under the heavy load of gasoline. Leaving the runway, the plane lifted off the ground and managed to clear a row of homes, the last barrier before soaring out of sight above the misty Pacific. Thus began the historic 7,332-nautical-mile journey.

Twenty-seven hours and more than 1,700 nautical miles later, the plane landed at Wheeler Field, Hawaii, where the crewmen were greeted by thousands of Hawaiians. The aviators refueled and took off again for another flight across the trackless ocean to Suva in the Fiji Islands, an area that no plane had ever flown before.

Then their troubles began. The crew fought a tropical storm; the engine began misfiring; the radio died and the compass failed. A slight error in navigation would have sent the crew into oblivion.

Thirty-four hours later the men finally reached Suva, where the entire population of 10,000 was out in the streets to honor the *Southern Cross* and her crew.

On June 8, the crew lifted off from Naselai Beach, 20 miles east of Suva, and began the final portion of its flight to Australia, the shortest leg of the journey, and wound its way over the open sea headed for the "land down under."

Only minutes off the ground, the first sign of trouble came when clouds covered the moon and the temperature dropped. In the middle of thunder, lightning and torrential rains, the wet and cold crewmembers fought to keep the plane under control during this most perilous part of the journey.

The next morning, and 21 hours and 18 minutes later, with a line of violet hills and brown cliffs unrolling along the western horizon, the Eagle Farm Aerodrome came into sight, along with 15,000 cheering people waiting to greet the men. The *Southern Cross* came in for a perfect landing, thus completing the world's first trans-Pacific flight, one of the most remarkable flights in history.

After the plane landed in Brisbane, Smithy was handed a cable from Captain Hancock congratulating the crew. The cable not only quitclaimed the plane to Smithy, but also released him from all indebtedness.

Smithy responded by radioing back: "Now that we are sure of success, we wish to announce to the world that we could never have made this flight without the generosity and wonderful help given us by Captain Allan Hancock. For months we had fought against giving up all hope, and we were practically counted out when we met Captain Hancock, who in a most unselfish manner saw us through."

On July 8, 1930, the *Southern Cross* came home to Hancock Field in Santa Maria, where Captain Hancock and acting mayor W. Walter Stokes, plus a crowd of cheering Santa Marians, were waiting to greet the crew.

Convinced that their plane could take them anywhere, Smithy and Ulm continued to fly the *Southern Cross,* many times in death-defying circumstances.

In May of 1935 the *Southern Cross,* piloted again by Smithy, made its last flight. Running dangerously out of oil and descending fast, it was saved by the heroic efforts of the co-pilot and navigator, P. G. Taylor.

Six months after the last flight of the *Southern Cross,* during a flight from England to Australia in the Lockheed Altair *Lady Southern Cross,* Smithy apparently met with bad weather while flying over the Bay of Bengal. When the plane failed to arrive in Singapore, an intense search was made, but neither the plane nor its crew was ever found.

Some years later the *Southern Cross* was given to the Australian National Museum; today it is on display at the Sir Charles Kingsford-Smith Memorial in Brisbane. In 1945 it was used in the making of a motion picture entitled *Smithy.*

A scale model of the *Southern Cross* is on display at the Santa Maria Valley Historical Society.

Frank Shields

E WAS THE EPITOME of old-time banking, answered to no one except himself, and knew everything about everyone—especially those who came to his bank for a loan.

Never in the history of local banking was there anyone more feared and respected than Frank Shields, the man who served as Vice President and Manager of the Santa Maria branch of the Bank of America until his retirement in 1964.

Frank Shields, who was born December 18, 1898, in Brady Island, Nebraska, began his long career in banking in 1918, when he served as bookkeeper at the Commercial Bank in Paxton, Nebraska. Four years later he came to California and took a position as utility clerk for A. P. Giannini's Bank of North Long Beach. Two years later the Long Beach bank became the Bank of Italy, and later, the Bank of America.

In 1924 Shields moved into the auditing department, spending much of his time traveling up and down the state inspecting the various banks owned by Mr. Giannini.

When Shields' report severely criticized the operations of the Santa Maria Branch, James L.

Glines, the branch manager, phoned the head office in San Francisco asking L. M. Giannini to "send that inspector up here" to see what he could do about straightening the place up.

Frank Shields reported for work in Santa Maria on December 11, 1928, and became Assistant Manager of the branch in December of 1931. After James Glines was killed in an auto accident in the early 1930s, Shields became Manager. He was promoted to Vice President and Manager in 1951.

Frank was honest and above-board, had a reputation of being "up front" with people, and expected everyone with whom he dealt to do the same.

Although a request for a loan was usually granted, the applicant knew that he'd be subjected to a long lecture, one that everyone in the bank could hear, as when Frank Shields spoke, everyone heard him. At the same time, however, he'd be writing up the loan papers.

Even though the man ruled his roost, hardworking dairymen and farmers could count on Frank to help them out, but he expected straight answers.

He typed (or wrote) up the loans on whatever pieces of paper were available and, if the borrower needed money in a hurry, he could get the loan papers processed by Frank in about five minutes. Again, though, as the man was writing up the loan, he'd subject the borrower to his usual loud lecture of how to run his business, what to do and how to do it! He never needed approval from higher sources, for, as far as the bank was concerned, he *was* the higher source.

In keeping with the bank's policy of having its officers sitting in desks where people could see them, Frank's desk was out front. Saturday mornings found crowds of people lined up to "hold court" with Shields.

Although he tried to help people who were having difficulties in repaying their loans, he wasn't shy about reminding them that they were behind in their payments. Again, he was not soft-spoken.

Frank came across as being gruff and outspoken, but he was a very sensitive man with a heart of gold. His friends tried not to sit next to him during weddings and funerals, since his loud sobbing prevented them from hearing the services. The man dearly loved his family and had a sincere interest in everyone's welfare. He was always on hand to give advice to his nieces and nephews— whether they asked for it or not. Every Sunday, after attending Mass at St. Mary of the Assumption Church, members of the Shields family of Santa Maria piled into station wagons for their weekly breakfast get-together at the Far Western Tavern in Guadalupe. Family time was important to the man.

Frank's sister, Margaret, was a registered nurse who came to Santa Maria to be near her brothers Frank and Ray after serving as an Army nurse in Denver. She became Superintendent of Nurses at the County Hospital, which was then located on West Morrison Avenue. She later married Denzil "Denny" Glines, who ranched in the Cuyamas. Ray worked as a bookkeeper for the Harry Heller Packing Company.

Frank Shields had many interests, particularly when young people were concerned. He paid them for their winning efforts at the County Fair by having his bank put up the prize money so that the winners could be paid immediately. He was also instrumental in starting the local Little League organization.

As an active member of Elks Lodge #1538, Frank was one of a group of members who initiated the Elks Rodeo in 1944, and was actively involved in advertising the event.

A meeting with 16 fellow members of the Elks lodge in 1943 resulted in each of them contributing $500 towards the founding of the Santa Maria Indians semi-pro baseball team. Frank served as chairman of its board of directors until 1952.

A few months before his official retirement in December of 1964, more than 350 friends and business associates, civic leaders and customers gathered at the Santa Maria Club to attend the testimonial barbecue dinner in honor of Frank Shields. His friends presented him with a $2500 ticket for a trip around the world, a trip to be taken after he officially retired from the Bank of America at the end of the year.

Thomas Weldon, Santa Maria Attorney and long-time friend of Shields, was the Master of Ceremonies. Speakers included Mayor C. Clayton Kyle; Supervisor Curtis Tunnell; former Santa Barbara Mayor John Rickard; and L. F. Lavagnino, who for many years had served as Shields' Assistant Manager.

Members of the celebration's barbecue team, all long-time personal friends of Shields, included A. B. Hanson, Owen Rice, Ernest Righetti, John Adam and Milo Ferini.

Samuel Stewart, chief legal counsel of the Bank of America, announced that when Shields returned from his trip, the bank would be providing him with an office where his Santa Maria friends could visit him for advice—"which, I'm certain, will be available at the same rate as in the past." However, this was an offer that Shields turned down, feeling that his being there would be an imposition to the man who would be replacing him.

After his retirement, Shields continued living at the Santa Maria Club and maintained his involvement in the local Elks organization as an honorary life member, as well as remaining prominent in the Chamber of Commerce, the Rotary Club and the Knights of Columbus.

Every morning, at the crack of dawn, Shields donned his regular business attire and proceeded to take a brisk walk around the town.

One of the most powerful men that the city has ever known, Frank Shields passed away in January of 1976 in his room at the Santa Maria Club. He is buried in the Santa Maria Cemetery next to his wife, Sybil, who died in 1955.

In the ensuing years, various people have reported seeing the figure of a man in the Santa Maria Club building (now the Landmark)—sitting at the bar smoking a cigar, or in a few cases, in the upstairs rooms. The vision has appeared only for a short time before disappearing. In every case, the description of the man has matched that of Frank Shields. The man who devoted so much of his efforts to Santa Maria just couldn't seem to leave the town that he loved so much. 🕸

George Mearns Scott

EORGE SCOTT'S EDUCATION ended and his career in insurance began when his father passed away and he had to go to work to help support his mother as well as his younger sister and brother.

George Mearns Scott, grandson of the Reverend William Anderson Scott, founder of both St. John's Presbyterian Church in San Francisco and the theological seminary in San Anselmo, was born in San Francisco in 1878.

When his father passed away, young Scott's hopes of ever attending college were dashed. He went to work for Aetna Insurance, where he remained until his siblings had reached adulthood and his mother had died.

In 1908, after serving with the National Guard during the great San Francisco earthquake, Scott decided to leave the Bay area and accept the invitation of his uncle and aunt, the Finleys, to come and live with them in Santa Maria.

When the oil companies were hiring workers for the rapidly growing oil industry, Scott went out to work for the Western Oil Company in the fields at Bicknell. He stayed with the company, living in one of the boarding houses in Orcutt, before buying out a small insurance business in Santa Maria.

A self-taught man, Scott compensated for his lack of a college degree by learning as much as he could, and built his little business up to where he was selling insurance, real estate and securities, and doing accounting work as well.

In 1915 Scott married Hattie Hart in San Rafael, and the two spent their honeymoon at Lake Tahoe. When they returned to Santa Maria, they made their home with Hattie's father, Reuben Hart, in his house at 606 South Broadway. After the property was sold to the city and the house was torn down, the Scotts moved to a house on East Camino Colegio.

When World War I broke out and Scott tried to enlist in the Army, the government kept turning him down. Finally, after deciding that his age might be against him, he dedicated his efforts to heading the local Red Cross facility.

During his spare time, Scott maintained both a vegetable and flower garden in back of his house. His dahlias always won prizes during the local flower shows.

He loved sports activities and took a great interest in local athletics, always bringing along a stopwatch when he attended the swimming meets at the Santa Maria Plunge. He took his two daughters to the opening day ceremonies of the 1932 Olympics at the Coliseum in Los Angeles, the year that Santa Maria's John Paulsen competed in the swimming contests.

George Scott was well liked and respected by both the young and old. He had a special talent of always making sure that when things were started, they were finished.

Having a lifelong interest in civic and community affairs, Scott became director of the Santa Maria Building and Loan Association in 1927, a position that he held until he passed away. He was a charter member of the Santa Maria Rotary Club, was a member of the County Fair Board for

George M. Scott family, mid-1920s. From left, Hattie Hart Scott, Elizabeth Hart Scott, Harriet Ann Scott, and George Mearnes Scott.

several years and served on the draft board during World War II.

George Scott insisted that his children obtain the college education that he never had. His two daughters, Betty and Ann, both graduated from the University of California—Betty at Berkeley and Ann at Los Angeles.

In January of 1963, at the age of 85, and two years after retiring from the insurance business, George Mearns Scott passed away. His wife, Hattie, died in January of 1978. Both are buried in the Santa Maria Cemetery.

Sadie West

OHN FRANK WEST, who had come to Santa Maria in 1888 with his parents, John and Harriet West, attended both Washington and Agricola grade schools, as did his sister, Ethel. On December 30, 1903, he married Sadie Wood at Nipomo.

After working as a blacksmith, John opened West's Battery shop in Santa Maria and later operated the local Ford agency, a position that he held until he passed away in July of 1931.

John was a quiet and unassuming man, but Sadie was just the opposite. She had come to the Santa Maria Valley long before women had the right to vote, and not only lived long enough to see women's suffrage become a reality, but served as the first woman to be elected to the Santa Maria City Council.

Sadie, one of Leonidas and Mary Wood's nine children, was born in Concordia, Kansas, on March 3, 1876, and moved to Glendale in 1883. She later came to Nipomo, where she met John West.

In 1909, after her doctor advised her to get out and get some fresh air, the saucy lady purchased a horse and buggy and set out to sell some farmland.

When John and Sadie moved to 800 North Broadway in Santa Maria in 1912 (where she also maintained a real estate office), there were only five other real estate agents in town, and all of them were men. In spite of her competition, Sadie proceeded to "set them all back on their heels" when she sold five pieces of real estate in one week.

Sadie continued selling real estate, only taking a break when her daughter, Lavona Ione, went to Los Angeles to attend college. Sadie, believing that no young girl should live alone in the big city, went with her. After returning to Santa Maria, Sadie resumed her real estate practice, working primarily with oil leases and developing property that she owned. She later formed her own drilling company and developed successful wells here in the valley, Cat Canyon, and later in New Mexico.

Sadie West was elected to the City Council in 1930 for a four-year term, defeating Bill Johnson, whose campaign slogan read: "Women aren't business people." Although Sadie proceeded to prove him wrong, it wasn't easy.

Her first appointment to the council's library committee met with little success, and her recommendations for library improvements were turned down, mainly because the projected cost of $1,300 exceeded the budget allowance for that particular fiscal year.

Since this was the time of the Great Depression, and both work and money were scarce, Sadie proposed that the city clean up Buena Vista Park and ease the unemployment problem by hiring some of the men who were out of work.

With Sadie's election to the Council coming not too long after women received the right to vote, men conceded that Women's Suffrage was a reality. However, they were adamant that women should not be working and "taking jobs away from men!"

The fact that Sadie was not only a shrewd businessperson, but a Council Member as well, was an irritating factor to the rest of the members. Since she was assigned jobs that would keep her "out of the way," she was unable to accomplish much, and the proposals that she made were generally voted down. However, it was during her term in office that City Hall was built.

When she suggested running a street parallel with Broadway in order to ease future traffic congestion, the council members chided: "You won't live long enough to see more traffic than Broadway can handle."

Even though she was defeated in the election of 1934, Sadie continued to take an active interest in civic affairs by attending all public meetings and never hesitating to voice her opinions. Generally remembered as a determined woman who never hesitated to stand up for what she believed in, Sadie was definitely ahead of her time.

Although she became active in a few of the local women's clubs and was considered to be a "go-getter," she spent most of her time running her real estate business.

In April of 1959, Sadie was honored for having served in the real estate business for 50 years. However, age had taken its toll and she was in poor health. After spending much time in and out of hospitals, Sadie passed away the following November, leaving her daughter, Lavona Ione Markling of Santa Maria, and two grandchildren, Mrs. Phyllis Ione Beach of Santa Ana and Paul Markling of Santa Maria. She is buried next to her husband, John, in the Santa Maria Cemetery.

For seventy years Sadie West remained on record as having been the only woman ever to serve on Santa Maria's City Council, a record that was broken by Alice Patino in the year 2000. 🎗️

Robert Valentine Higgins

LTHOUGH SANTA MARIA is recognized as having produced noteworthy people in almost every walk of life, with many going on to great distinction, one can probably count on the fingers of one hand the numbers of those who turned their backs on fame and fortune and returned to their roots.

After Adelia and Louis Higgins moved to Santa Maria during the early part of the 20th century and farmed on the 600 block of West Fesler, their five children attended local schools and graduated from Santa Maria High School. Only Edna and Bob pursued higher education.

The year after Edna earned her master's degree from Columbia in 1912, she married James F. Strachan, and eventually became a widely known writer of stage and radio plays. She became women's editor of the *Daily Californian* and literary editor of *The Occident.* She later served as president of the Berkeley Play-makers.

Upon graduation from high school, Bob Higgins enrolled in Stanford University, majoring in Drama and English, and graduated in 1916. The following year he enrolled in the Academy of Dramatic Arts in New York, where he studied for one year.

Bob chose to stay in New York for a few years where he was involved with the acting community on Broadway and appeared in two productions with Mae West while also writing short stories and verse for magazines. One of his sonnets, "Western Harvest," was included in Edwin Markham's 1926 *Anthology.*

Why Bob chose to give up his Broadway career isn't clear, but he returned to Santa Maria, where he became a teacher of Drama and English at Santa Maria High School. He remained at the school until 1948, when he retired.

Bob Higgins, brother of Barbara Mussell, is remembered as being a generally nice guy, mostly noted for his easy going and friendly disposition. His sense of humor and stories about life on Broadway contributed to making his drama class one of the most popular at the school.

During the 23 years that Bob served at the high school, he earned the distinction of

PHOTO COURTESY OF AUDREY AND DOUGLAS MUSSELL

directing most of the senior plays, some of which his sister had written. Her play, *The McMurray Chin,* a Senior Class and Junior College joint production of 1931, included in its cast Irene Donovan, Norman Johnson, Maret Duthie, Bob Mason, Nona Vaughn, Norma Pine, Lois Mendenhall, Margaret Fesler, Dorothy Wharff, Norman Coy and Kenneth Crossman.

Other high school actors directed by Higgins and Ethel Pope included just about everyone in his English and Drama classes. After graduating from high school, many of his former students joined the Santa Maria Players Club, where they again acted under the direction of their former drama teacher.

Although Higgins directed the senior class productions, his talents weren't limited to high school plays. He wrote, directed and acted in some of the Players Club productions, as well as those in Berkeley and his Alma Mater, Stanford.

After retiring from teaching in June of 1948, Higgins continued to write poetry, his labor of love. The year following his retirement, the Decker Press of Prairie City, Illinois, published his book of poems, *Sub Rosa.*

In March of 1950, Robert Higgins received a letter from Cyril Coniston Clemens (third cousin, twice removed, of Samuel Langhorne Clemens), advising him that he'd been nominated to honorary membership in the International Mark Twain Society. Mr. Clemens had formed this group in 1930 for "the purpose of knitting the whole world in bonds of cultured peace."

Often called "The League of Nations of Literature," honorary membership in the group was conferred to those entitled, in the opinion of the society, to recognition in various fields, such as drama, music, poetry, arts or films. The Mark Twain Medal has been awarded to such notables as Winston Churchill, Lady Nancy Astor, Harry Truman, Clement Atlee, Clare Boothe Luce, Herbert Hoover, Franklin Delano Roosevelt, George Bernard Shaw, William Marconi, John Pershing, Oliver Wendell Holmes and many other people whose names could have been listed in *Who's Who in the World.*

Sadly, Higgins' health began to deteriorate and he was diagnosed as having Parkinson's disease.

On January 19, 1956, Robert Valentine Higgins, at 64 years of age, passed away in the Santa Maria Hospital. His ashes are buried in Mussell Fort.

John Paulsen

"OHN PAULSEN, Santa Maria's breaststroke swimming hope for the American Olympic team, is working out in the long outdoor Olympiad pool in Los Angeles.

"Young Paulsen will be sent to Cincinnati next month to compete for a place on the American Olympic squad if enough money is subscribed by his friends here."

In 1925, when Bill Paulsen left a creamery in Fresno to work for the Santa Maria Creamery and Cheese Factory, he moved his wife and four children, Margaret Ellen, Dorothy, Carl and John, into a home located next door to the Hobbs family.

As neighbors, George Hobbs and Carl Paulsen became good friends, a friendship that continued until the mid-sixties, when Carl, then living in Taylorsville, died of cancer.

John Paulsen, the eldest of four children, was a member of the Santa Maria High School swimming team, a team which traveled throughout the state, participating in one meet after another and collecting trophies along the way.

Because of Paul Nelson's expert coaching, and with Charles Taylor as training supervisor, the stars of the swimming team became internationally known swimmers, with Paulsen, Cassius Purkiss, Roger Hatch, and Allan Stewart forming the nucleus of this powerful team.

Without a doubt, the 1932 swimming team was one of the best in the history of the school.

In April of 1932, when three swimmers

from the school's swimming team were sent to Los Angeles to participate in the dedication of the new Olympic Swimming Stadium, John Paulsen took

first place in the 100-meter breaststroke event, a win which decided the Southern California AAU championship for that year. In that same year, young Paulsen astonished the swimming world when he set a new world interscholastic mark in the 100-yard breaststroke in 1 minute, 7.07 seconds.

In holding several records in the breaststroke, Paulsen was rated among the best on the Pacific Coast.

Paulsen originally went to the Olympic trials as an alternate, but wound up as one of the 21 breaststroke swimmers from 12 different countries seeking the gold medal in the 200-meter breaststroke event.

Although the day was sweltering hot, more than 100 Santa Marians stood among the 105,000 spectators waiting to welcome the Olympic hopefuls as they marched into the Olympic Stadium. When Paulsen passed by, along with the rest of the extraordinarily large American contingent, his 6-foot, 4-inch frame seemed to vibrate with the spirit of America's will to win.

At 17 years of age, John was reported to be one of the youngest swimmers on the American team.

Alas, in spite of the extra personal coaching of Paul Nelson, young Paulsen's hopes were dashed when the Japanese teams surprised the world and ran away with many of the medals, including John's 200-meter breaststroke event.

After the Olympics competition ended, John returned to Santa Maria to complete his high school education.

During his high school years Paulsen had won the National Breaststroke Championship, plus two second-place National A.A.U. Breaststroke championships, one in the Long Beach Swimming Stadium and one in the Hawaiian Swimming and Diving Stadium at Waikiki Beach in Oahu, Hawaii.

John graduated from Santa Maria High School in June of 1933, and with the help of Francis McGinley, a former Santa Maria High School football star who attended USC and was a member of the university's football team, John obtained a swimming scholarship to that prestigious university.

John entered the USC School of Business in 1933, and, along with many other athletes, worked his way through college by waiting on tables, gardening, parking cars and working as an extra in a few motion pictures. With the country being in the depths of the Great Depression, money was a scarce commodity, and people worked at any job they could get.

During his four years at USC, John was a member of the school's swimming and water polo teams which competed against both eastern and western universities.

Paulsen graduated from USC in June of 1937 with a Bachelor's Degree in Business and began working with the Union Pacific Railroad in Omaha, Nebraska, in marketing the company's new resort in Sun Valley, Idaho. During the course of his employment he traveled to various cities in the eastern United States, soliciting sportsmen guests for the resort's summer and winter events.

During John's employment with Union Pacific, he applied for admission to the U. S. Navy for officer's training.

After six months training in the Naval School at Northwestern University in Chicago, he received his commission as Ensign in the U. S. Naval Reserves and was assigned to the Navy Mine Sweeping Detail at Pearl Harbor, with duties at various locations in the Pacific.

On March 3, 1944, John, then a Lieutenant, was assigned to a large new aircraft carrier, the USS *Ticonderoga,* a vessel which was soon to be commissioned at Newport News, Virginia, and assigned to the Pacific Fleet.

As assistant navigator, John was a part of the

Ticonderoga's many heroic operations in the Pacific Theater until two Japanese kamikaze bombers hit the ship in April of 1945. The ship, suffering severe damage, was taken to the Naval Yard in Bremerton, Washington, for repairs.

John's next assignment was as navigator aboard the new USS *Saidor*, another aircraft carrier which was scheduled to be commissioned to carry a special Marine Corps air group on its planned attack on the Japanese mainland.

In August of 1945 the United States dropped atomic bombs on Hiroshima and Nagasaki, and the war came to an end.

John served aboard the *Saidor* until he was detached from the Navy on April 18, 1946, after serving a period of four and a half years.

After leaving the Navy, John began working as a salesman in the San Francisco division of the St. Regis Paper Company, a position that he held until retirement, when he and his wife, Gloria moved to San Ramon.

John Paulsen, the first athlete from Santa Maria to compete in the Olympics (and who had once delivered newspapers for the *Santa Maria Times*) maintained friendships throughout the years with several of his friends in Santa Maria. ❧

The Gatewood Family

N 1932, WHEN Homer Messina needed an assistant for his barbershop in Santa Maria, he contacted Louden Gatewood, who was then working in a shoe shine shop in Bakersfield. Gatewood came to town, liked what he saw, accepted the position and immediately began working at Messina's shop. The following December, he moved his family to Santa Maria.

M. Louden Gatewood, son of a man born into slavery, was born in Pueblo, Colorado, in 1900, and moved to Needles, California, while still a boy. During his early years he learned to shine shoes, an occupation that was destined to support him for the rest of his life.

Because work in his chosen profession was scarce, Mr. Gatewood often found it necessary to move to different areas, wherever work was available. In 1926 he moved to Chehalis, Washington, where he met and married Eula Mae Whiteside. In 1932, the Gatewoods and their three children moved to Bakersfield, where two more children were born.

Two years after arriving in Santa Maria, Gatewood left Messina's shop and opened a shoe shine parlor in the old ticket booth of the Gaiety theater on West Main Street near McClelland. From the West Main Street site he opened the Gatewood Shine Parlor on South Broadway between Church and West Main Street, approximately where the Bank of America is located today.

Louden Gatewood's shine parlor on South Broadway, 1936

At first, shoe shining was the only service that Gatewood offered. However, by 1938 he was selling magazines, books, cigarettes, tobacco, candy and popcorn.

During World War II, when soldiers from the various military installations came into the shop to get their shoes shined, Gatewood's shop was open twelve hours a day, seven days a week. With both Clyde and Leroy helping their father shine shoes and Annabelle working as cashier as well as keeping the business records, his shop prospered.

After the war ended, Gatewood closed the

shop, but, still needing to support his large family, he went to work for various businesses in Santa Maria. He and Eula both died in the 1950s and are buried in the Santa Maria Cemetery.

All of the Gatewood children attended local schools and were known throughout the Santa Maria area for their athletic ability as well as their participation in various school programs.

Clyde, the oldest child, entered the U. S. Navy shortly after graduating from Santa Maria High School in 1944. When the war ended and he was discharged, he worked as an electronics and aerospace engineer in the San Francisco and Los Angeles areas.

Annabelle, the second oldest child, graduated from Santa Maria High School in 1946 and from Santa Maria Junior College the following year. In 1947 she married Eric Tell, who owned his own trucking business. Annabelle passed away in April of 2001 at the age of 73.

Leroy, the third Gatewood child, unlike his brothers and sisters, never had the opportunity to participate in sports, as he was too busy working for his father. When he was old enough to work he became his father's right-hand man.

In addition to his working at the shoe shine shop, during World War II he delivered the *Santa Maria Times*. He also had the responsibility of telling people on his block to turn off their lights during the periodic blackouts. Since paper routes were considered to be a part of the war effort, Leroy received special permission from the government to purchase a bicycle.

Leroy was drafted into the military and served with the Army for two years before returning to Santa Maria. He worked for Souza's Music Center, staying there for 25 years until the business closed. Leroy passed away in 1996.

Urelalee was born in Bakersfield and attended Santa Maria schools. Several years after graduating from Santa Maria High School, she married Connie Seymore and moved to Guadalupe, where she lived until her death in 1978.

Leander Gatewood, born in Bakersfield, was only five months old when his family moved to Santa Maria. As a dedicated Boy Scout, Leander became the first black Eagle Scout in Santa Maria. At that time he had won more awards than any other Boy Scout on the Central Coast. In addition to being named to the Order of the Arrow fraternal organization and being a charter member of the Northern Santa Barbara chapter, he also became a Sea Explorer Scout, serving as assistant skipper aboard a Sea Scout ship sponsored by the American Legion.

After graduating from Santa Maria High School in 1950, he continued his education at both Santa Maria Junior College and Hancock College. He also played football with the Santa Maria Valley Athletic Club's Redskins.

Leander chose to make the Army his career after being drafted into the Army during the Korean conflict. He served two tours of duty in the Republic of Vietnam, earning the Bronze Star Medal. He retired at the age of 43 as first sergeant after having served twenty-three years with the United States Army, and returned to the Central Coast, where he began working with the Orcutt Union School as director of maintenance, operations and transportation. He retired sixteen years later.

Geraldine Gatewood, the sixth Gatewood child, born March 21, 1935, in the Grigsby Hospital, then located in the 300 block of East Church Street, was the first black child born in the city of Santa Maria. After graduating from Santa Maria High School, she married Emmanuel Manson and moved to Northern California.

Norman, the Gatewoods' seventh child, worked in his father's shoeshine parlor and also served as a newspaper carrier with the *Santa Maria Times* in 1959. He later worked for the Roemer and Rubel Automotive dealership on

North Broadway. He played both trombone and drums with the high school's band, orchestra and dance band.

Being active in sports, he was voted "All-Conference Player of the Year" in high school football. After graduating from Santa Maria High School in 1955, he attended Hancock College, where he was voted "Most Valuable Player" on the Hancock College football team of 1956.

After serving with the U. S. Naval Reserve, he moved to the Los Angeles area.

Donald, the Gatewoods' eighth child, was active in all high school sports and became Santa Maria High School's first black student body president. After graduating from high school in 1957, Don received a football scholarship and entered Idaho State College. He worked for the city of Santa Maria from 1961 through 1965, and then taught and coached football at St. Joseph's High School until 1969. From 1970 through 1997, Don worked in various vocational schools in

Santa Maria as well as in Orange and Ventura counties. During this time he also earned a Business degree from the University of San Francisco.

Kenneth, the youngest Gatewood child, played in Little League in the 1950s while selling newspapers on street corners. After graduating from Santa Maria High School in 1961, he went to work for Unocal, a job that he held until he retired.

Life was difficult for the Gatewoods. The fingers on Louden's right hand never grew to normal length, but he refused to cater to his handicap. Both he and Eula were hard working people. Each of the Gatewood children, who learned responsibility, duty and dedication from Louden and Eula Mae, had the opportunity to seek higher education. Those who didn't receive scholarships worked their way through school.

The Gatewood family, the first black family to move to Santa Maria, lived at 204 East Church Street before moving to the 600 block of West Church Street. ❧

Don Gatewood

Paul Nelson

AUL LANCOURT NELSON, who was born in January of 1898 in Columbus, Ohio, came to Santa Maria in 1926 to take over the management of the Santa Maria Plunge, a new 20-yard pool located in the 600 block of South Broadway. In 1944 he went on to become the city's Recreation Director.

Although Paul had been a swimming star at the Los Angeles Athletic Club and still held many records for the breaststroke at the time of his death, he lacked the proper credentials for coaching at the high school level. However, he was directly responsible for the training of Santa Maria High School's swimmers, who were sent over to him by Charles "Doak" Taylor.

Paul was always on the lookout for natural talent. However, he didn't have to look far, as the Santa Maria High School students had more talent than could be found in most towns of similar size. With Paul's expertise, encouragement, and training, the boys were able to compete with world-class swimmers in the larger schools between San Francisco and Los Angeles.

The high school sent busloads of swimmers to such cities as Palo Alto and Fullerton, and to the California Interscholastic Federation competitions. Since these were mostly weekend meets, parents provided the transportation.

Paul was a tall, thin and conservatively dressed man who carried himself with dignity. He was so well-known and admired throughout California that famous swim clubs from the San Francisco and Los Angeles areas sent their agents to Santa Maria to talk with him.

He was strict, had a dry sense of humor, and had a sincere affection for his students. Many local young men, both swimmers and divers, became champion swimmers because Paul Nelson had personally coached them.

In one of his periodic columns for the *Santa Maria Daily Times*, Nelson described how Winston Johnson, when only 8 years of age, swam against some adult men swimmers, "paddling a great race across to win two cups." Norman Johnson "shocked the San Diego Athletic Club" when he won the 50-yard backstroke, competing against the club's former Pacific Coast backstroke champ. With humorous affection, he dubbed John Hatch the "free style expert" and Allen Stewart the "Diving Adonis." He also remembered watching over the balcony of the San Francisco Olympics as Cassius Purkiss paced John Weissmuller.

Although his swimming competition began after graduating from high school, Parnell Tilley, a free-style swimmer in open water, could beat anyone up and down the coast. He was on his way to being a world class swimmer when World War II came along. Dorwin Coy, Buddy Spears, Roger Hatch, Bert Gill, John Scaroni, Allan Stewart,

Rollo Crews . . . the list of great swimmers and divers from the Santa Maria area goes on and on.

John Paulsen, captain of the high school swimming team for four years, was Paul Nelson's most famous protégé and became the first Santa Marian to participate in the Olympics. During the 1930 Nationals at Long Beach, Paulsen placed second, ahead of some of the state's more famous swimmers.

Paul Nelson passed away on March 8, 1952, and his wife, Dorothea, who served as Santa Maria's librarian for 35 years, passed away in 1994.

The new city pool on South McClelland was named the "Paul Nelson Pool" on St. Patrick's Day of 1958, and was dedicated on the 17th of April of the following year. 🐚

Shortly after his arrival in California in 1926, Paul Nelson participated in an aquatic sport unavailable in his native Ohio.

Henry "Pat" Stubbs

HEN WORD WAS RECEIVED of the death of Henry E. "Pat" Stubbs in March of 1937, his friends were not surprised, as the much-liked and respected man had been seriously ill since suffering a heart attack the previous summer.

Pat was born March 4, 1881, near Coleman, Texas, where he received his primary education before enrolling in Phillips University in Enid, Oklahoma, to study for the ministry. After receiving his degree, he held pastorates in both Oklahoma and Texas before coming to California. In 1923, he moved from Tulare to Santa Maria, where he took over the duties of Pastor of the First Christian Church.

Pat made friends wherever he went, and always had the best interests of Santa Maria at heart. During the winter of 1931, while the country was in the depths of the Great Depression, he established a "soup kitchen" for the hungry.

He served the church almost nine years before being persuaded by his friends to enter the political field and run for the congressional seat of the Tenth District, then composed of Santa Barbara, San Luis Obispo, Tulare, Kern, and Ventura Counties.

Pat's campaign against Arthur Crites was remarkable. Campaigning vigorously day and night, often sleeping in his car while covering his district, this politically unknown minister with no campaign funds wound up as the district's first elected member to the House of Representatives.

When his many friends gathered at a farewell reception given just before he and his family left for Washington, Stubbs resolved to measure up to the trust that the people of this district had given him and hoped to take a small part in the destiny of the nation. "The government needs more devoted Christians in its service."

Two years later, Congressman Stubbs defeated George Bliss of Carpinteria in the general election. During that term in office he served on the House Irrigation and Reclamation Committee and the Public Lands and Indian Affairs Committees, both of the latter committees being of particular interest to the western states.

Shortly after the primaries covering his third nomination for the Congressional seat, Stubbs suffered a heart attack at his home on Orcutt Road and was taken to Airport Hospital, where he stayed for many weeks, receiving numerous blood transfusions. In spite of the fact that it was generally felt that he wouldn't recover, he went on to defeat Bliss again in the general election, receiving even more votes than he'd received in the two previous elections.

When Stubbs left for Washington early in December of 1936, his friends feared that he'd never return alive. Their fears were realized when, shortly after arriving in the nation's capital, Pat was taken to Walter Reed General Hospital, where the oath of office was administered to him when the new Congress assembled the following January. He never recovered.

On February 27, Mrs. Stubbs received a phone call from their son, Elbert, who was serving on his father's office staff, telling her that Pat was sinking fast. Although she and their daughter, Mrs. Andrea Faris of Shell Beach, left from San Luis Obispo the next day, Congressman Stubbs passed away, with his son at his side, before they could reach him.

Although Stubbs had suffered physical problems for some time, he was generally known as a hard worker and one who was much respected by his fellow Congressmen. His genial disposition, in spite of his physical discomforts, won him friends wherever he went. Through his untiring work he was able to do much to further the great Valley Reclamation Project. He secured many new federal buildings for his district, including a new Post Office, and was instrumental in locating many soil conservation projects and CCC camps in the district.

The body of Congressman Stubbs was returned to Santa Maria, where services were held on March 4 at the Stubbs home on Orcutt Road. Four of his fellow Congressmen attended the services. Burial followed at the Santa Maria Cemetery, within a tombstone that resembles that of the Unknown Soldier in Washington, D.C. Ruby Belle Stubbs passed away in September of 1952.

In 1962, when the redwood tree which had been planted in memory of Henry E. Stubbs during the dedication of the new Post Office on May 29, 1937, was scheduled to be cut down, Don Holser strongly felt that this was a tree that should be saved. With the help of nurseryman Burt Trick, A. J. Diani and the Engel and Gray Trucking Company, the tree was moved from the Post Office property to the Russell Avenue Park, where it still stands in memory of Pat Stubbs, the man who passed away in service as Santa Maria's first member of Congress of the Tenth Congressional District.

Flora Rivers

PHOTO COURTESY OF MR. AND MRS. ROBERT RIVERS

SOMETIMES, IN THE FACE of adversity, a person will rise to the occasion, take charge of the situation, and do whatever is necessary in spite of the hardships he or she may face. Santa Maria has had no shortage of such people whose stars have shone bright in spite of the odds.

Flora Rivers, who served as City Clerk from 1928 until she retired in 1944, met with what could have been a disastrous situation when her husband died as a result of a tragic accident, leaving her as the sole support of her four young children.

Flora Anne Lowdermilk, daughter of Henry and Helen Lowdermilk, was born on October 15, 1889, in North Carolina. A true member of American pioneer stock, her ancestors had come to this country from England prior to the Revolutionary War.

Miss Lowdermilk received her early education in the schools of Anadarko, Oklahoma, before enrolling in a business college in Phoenix, Arizona, where she took a secretarial course. Her education was destined to serve her well in the years to come.

Although Flora's first experience in the business world found her working in insurance and real estate offices in Phoenix, it was her later position as private secretary to both the Secretary of State and Surveyor General of the state of Arizona that gave her untold expertise in the public sector.

Shortly after her marriage to Arthur J. Rivers in December of 1911, the newlyweds moved to Los Angeles, where Arthur, Jr., was born in 1913. From Los Angeles, the Rivers family moved to Santa Barbara, where Ruth Virginia, Dorothy Anne and Robert W. were born. In 1918, when Bobby was one year old, the Rivers family moved to Santa Maria, where Mr. Rivers owned and operated the Cadillac dealership.

In August of 1923, Mr. Rivers was killed when he was hit by a train in the Los Angeles area. Shortly after his death, a representative from the Southern California head office of Cadillac dealerships came up to Santa Maria from Los Angeles, sold all of the cars on Mr. Rivers' lot, and gave the proceeds of the sales to the widow of the man who had served the company so capably. With no insurance to tide her over, this was a Godsend to Mrs. Rivers.

As a widow with four children, the youngest being only five years old, Mrs. Rivers faced dim prospects. However, always one to face problems head on, she obtained a position as stenographer at the Pacific Southwest Bank. Less than two years later she accepted a position as Frank McCoy's private secretary at the Santa Maria Inn, a position that she held for three years.

When Flora took Mr. McCoy's advice to run for the job of City Clerk, thereby challenging the incumbent, A. H. Drexler, not many people thought that she had a chance of winning. However, no one was aware of the fact that she had some of the strongest campaign workers in the city, as all four of her children pitched in to help. Bobby, who sold papers in the downtown area, carried her cards, which he passed out freely.

With very little money in the campaign chest, Flora's campaign team looked for ways to economize. When Virginia typed a letter which Flora had written to every voter in Santa Maria, Dorothy and Bobby hand-delivered them, thus saving the 3-cent postage fees. By today's standards, that may seem to be miserly, but at that time Mrs. Rivers was supporting her four children and needed every dime that she could make. Mr. Drexler, assuming that he would win by a landslide, didn't waste his time in campaigning at all.

In the primary election of June, 1928, to the surprise of everyone except her four children, Flora Rivers was elected to the position of City Clerk and Assessor for the city of Santa Maria, a position that she was destined to hold for sixteen years. Some say that she was the first woman to be elected to a paid elected municipal position in the state of California.

Having had extensive experience while working for Civil Service in Arizona, she stuck to the letter of the law. Even though some people didn't agree with her, they respected her for her knowledge and effectiveness. As time passed, some of her most ardent opponents began to support her.

While Mrs. Rivers was doing her job for the city, her daughter Virginia ran the house and took care of the rest of her siblings, a mighty big job for a girl who was less than 15 years old at the time.

Flora Rivers is remembered as being a capable person with a large circle of friends. When her son, Bobby, became a prisoner of war during World War II, she assisted the military by sending coded letters to him questioning the enemy's operations, etc. Bob, by using the same code, was able to funnel information back to the military through his mother.

During the time that Bob was being held in a German prisoner of war camp, Flora still served the city well and was re-elected time after time by a two-to-one margin.

Mrs. Rivers was as capable as she was personable. She had a deep interest in civic affairs and supported all causes for the betterment of the community.

On December 2, 1968, Flora Anne Rivers passed away at her home at 2059 Lockwood Lane in Santa Maria. She is buried in the family plot in a cemetery in Inglewood.

The Community Orchestra

 ECEMBER'S PRODUCTION of Engelbert Humperdinck's famous opera, *Hansel and Gretel,* was one of the main highlights of 1927. Because the opera, written in 1895, was reputed to be a difficult one to perform, few amateur productions of this world-renowned work had ever been attempted.

However, in spite of the opera's difficulties, the Santa Maria Community Orchestra's presentation of this work was a huge success, and much credit was given to the musical company by the local press. The main characters, played by Margaret Konarsky and Oliver Smith, brought down the house in the last act with a duet that was appropriately described in the *Santa Maria Times* as "a gem."

The Community Orchestra was a neighborly gathering, with its members representing a cross-section of the entire community. Robert Easton played the flute, while Captain G. Allan Hancock ("father of the orchestra") played the cello. Both Doctor and Mrs. Dan Sink participated in the group, as did Harriet Bigler.

After the last performance of this rousing success, the performers attended a cast party at the Santa Maria Club. The party was still going strong at 2 o'clock, when an announcement was made that a special train was scheduled to leave at 8 o'clock to carry supporters to witness the Santa Maria and Fullerton high school teams battle for the Southern California football championship. The merrymakers quickly left for home to catch a few winks before boarding the train for Los Angeles.

It wasn't long before the orchestra's reputation spread throughout the Central Coast and the group was asked to perform in many of the surrounding cities. After a performance in San Luis Obispo with Lillian E. Ferguson as featured soprano and Mary Angell as pianist, the city's local newspapers wrote, "You have shown us what can be done through a labor of love for the better things in music, and we thank you and hope you may come again soon."

On the 22nd of May in 1928, representatives of the Community Orchestra, Players Club, Harmony Club and those interested in opera production met in the studio of radio station KSMR to discuss the advisability of forming a Community Arts Association within the city. The group wrote a tentative constitution along with bylaws for the association. Conductor Strobridge noted that he believed it to be "an absolute necessity for the various art groups in Santa Maria to form some sort of federation whereby mutual interests would be cared for and which would foster and encourage artistic endeavor on more extensive lines."

Meanwhile, the people of the valley continued to be enthralled with its Community Orchestra. *The Marriage of Figaro* was the first production to be broadcast over the new remote control set of station KSMR from microphones installed in the orchestra pit. The production, directed by Arnold A. Bowhay, gave unending pleasure to its audience. The familiar voices of Julia Smith, William Matchan, Oliver Smith and Lillian Ferguson thrilled Santa Marians. The *Times* reported that the ensemble members were more effective because of the voices of Arthur Amaral, Wesley Hatch and Chester Cox.

In February of 1932, the Santa Maria Opera association, along with the Santa Maria Community Orchestra, presented Bizet's four-part opera *Carmen* in the high school auditorium. Julia Beeson Smith played the role of Carmen, with tenor Morton Scott playing the part of Don José. The *Times* praised the singing of Ethel Mae Dorsey, who played the part of Micaëla, while Charles Wesley Hatch played the role of Zuniga, captain of the soldiers.

The first concert of the year was held in the Presbyterian Church auditorium in May of 1935, with Sydney Peck directing and George Yeary serving as concertmaster. Although some of the original musicians continued to be a part of the orchestra, new names appeared on the program, a

true indication of the valley's commitment to its community orchestra.

The Community Orchestra, which was in existence from 1925 to 1935, ended when Allan Hancock began to send his people, who had come to the Santa Maria Valley to operate his various enterprises, to businesses elsewhere. Since many of these people were professional musicians, the vacancies created within the orchestra could not be filled by local musicians.

However, while the Community Orchestra was in its prime, the city illustrated to the highest degree what cooperation would accomplish in the success of an endeavor. The orchestra, which began as weekly social musical get-togethers, progressed to a high state of musical performance which not only cemented the friendships of the people of the community, but also furnished its supporters with untold pride and enjoyment. 🌸

Wataru Sutow

LTHOUGH HE WASN'T well known outside the medical field, the contributions that he made in cancer research resulted in some of the most dramatic treatment of the disease in the history of pediatric oncology.

From his earliest days, people who knew Wataru Sutow somehow sensed that there was something special about the boy and that he would some day make his mark on the world.

Yasaku and Yoshi Sutow were two of the first Japanese people to settle in Hawaii before finally coming to San Francisco and then down to Guadalupe, where Sutow began growing flowers for seed, specializing in nasturtiums. Both their sons, Wataru and Masao, were born in Guadalupe.

Wataru, who was born on August 31, 1912, didn't start school until he was nine years old. Seven years later, at the age of sixteen, he graduated as class valedictorian from Santa Maria High School, completing the four-year course of study in three years. Sadly, his father passed away two weeks before he graduated.

Although Wataru took his studies seriously, he had other interests as well. During his high school years he was an outstanding baseball player, playing outfield for both the high school and the Buddhist Church teams. He also learned the art of magic, and often performed magic shows with his close friend Ralph Adams, who graduated from Santa Maria High School in 1932.

While attending high school in Santa Maria, Sutow applied for and received a scholarship to Stanford University. When he ran out of money with which to meet his living expenses at Standford, he took a four-year leave of absence and worked as a bookkeeper for Setsuo Aratani's Guadalupe Produce Company. He later returned to the university, where he resumed his studies in medicine.

When World War II disrupted his studies at Stanford, Sutow moved to Northeastern Medical School in Illinois and later entered Utah University Medical School, where he received his M.D. degree in 1944.

In 1948, the year after he'd moved to Los Angeles to practice medicine, he joined the Atomic Bomb Casualty Commission (ABCC) in Hiroshima, Japan, where he served as Chief of Pediatrics, studying the effects of radiation from the atomic bomb on children. He left the Commission in 1950 and moved his family back to the United States, settling in Redwood City in order to finish his residency at the Stanford University School of Medicine.

In 1951 Sutow was drafted into the Army. He took his basic training at San Antonio, Texas, and Camp Roberts, California. While he was en route to Europe, the Army issued orders for him to return to Hiroshima, where he was again assigned to the Atomic Bomb Casualty Commission. From 1952 to 1954, he traveled back and forth between Hiroshima and Nagasaki, again studying the effects and treatment of radiation on the young survivors of the atomic bomb. At the end of his tour of duty in Japan, every cancer research university in the United States wanted him on its staff.

In 1954, Dr. Sutow accepted a position with the world-famous cancer research hospital, the University of Texas M. D. Anderson Cancer Center in Houston, Texas, where his initiative and innovations helped to convert a tiny four-bed corner in a ward to a full-fledged pediatrics center.

With surgery and radiation being the only treatments of choice at the time, Dr. Sutow, convinced that chemotherapy could be an effective treatment for cancer in children, faced an uphill battle against popular opinion.

In addition to his innovations in helping to make Wilm's Tumor one of the most curable of childhood solid tumors, his treatment of osteosarcoma resulted in survival rates of more than 60%. Prior to the use of chemotherapy, the cure rate had only been 20%. Breakthroughs such as these led to similar studies for other forms of cancer.

Although remembered as a good conversationalist, Sutow was a complex man, according to his wife, Mary. He rarely talked, but he was a good listener.

Remembered as a "knowing and gentle man," Sutow was particularly noted for his ability to sight-read, or to understand an entire paragraph without reading it word-for-word, thus enabling him to read volumes of material in a short time. Still, though, he was a compassionate man and built unforgettable rapport with his patients. Young patients eagerly awaited the doctor's evening rounds ("roundup time"), and offered hands and feet for him to decorate with a flower or butterfly drawn with his ball-point pen. These decorations, of course, were lost in the child's next confrontation with soap and water.

Although his magician days were over, Dr. Sutow still maintained other interests. He collected and studied seashells, and was fascinated by the growth and development of these shells just as he was by the same processes in children. He later had some of them x-rayed in order to show the intricate patterns in shell structure.

According to a publication by the M. D. Anderson Hospital, Dr. Sutow wrote more than 250 articles and reports on the treatment of childhood cancer and contributed material to about 20 textbooks during the course of his career. These publications and his fight to change existing attitudes about the treatment of childhood cancer led to the creation of the W. W. Sutow Visiting Professorship in Pediatric Oncology at the M. D. Anderson Hospital, a professorship that was established after the doctor's death. In 1976 he received the Heath Memorial Award for his outstanding care of patients with cancer.

In spite of Dr. Sutow's lifetime work in cancer research, his own personal battle with the disease was lost. After serving 27 years at the famous hospital and research center, Dr. Wataru W. Sutow died of cancer at the M. D. Anderson Hospital on December 20, 1981.

Funeral services were held at the Buddhist Church in Guadalupe, and he was interred in the Guadalupe Cemetery next to his parents.

In reminiscing about Dr. Sutow, Ralph Adams, the popular local school photographer and lifetime friend of the doctor, said, "When you needed a friend, 'Wat' was there. He was, without a doubt, the best friend I've ever had."

Hancock West Point of the Air

In this group of flight instructors at the Hancock Foundation College of Aeronautics, Thomas Penfield is sixth from left in the top row.

I N MAY OF 1939, with war clouds gathering throughout the world, Captain Allan Hancock was among eight flying school operators summoned to Washington by General Henry H. "Hap" Arnold, Chief of the Army Air Corps.

Arnold, in addressing the group, came right to the point. The Corps desperately needed pilots, but the government lacked the means with which to provide the training. When he asked the men to contract with the government to provide such training, Captain Hancock was one of the first to agree to the request. From that time on, all of the captain's energies, experience and facilities were centered on the country's defense effort.

In 1940, the Hancock College of Aeronautics, acting as one of the private contractors to the United States government while under the direction of military officers, provided a ground school and primary training for the Army Air Corps. By the time World War II ended in 1945, civilian school contractors had trained more than 200,000 pilots for the Army, thereby saving the government $1 billion in that particular phase of the war effort.

The Hancock Foundation College of Aeronautics, the first non-profit school of its kind in the country, opened its doors to train young pilots in May of 1929, and was hailed as the future West Point of the Air.

Always looking for perfection, Capt. Hancock

brought in the country's top flight instructors so that the boys going through his system would be the best pilots in the sky. In addition to E. A. Blanchard, P. A. Ross, J. A. Bachelder, and D. E. Stanford and other pilots teaching at the school, in 1940 Hancock hired Thomas Penfield from the Bay area.

Penfield, who was born in the San Diego area, grew up in Paradise. He took his first lessons in flying in 1923 at the age of 26, paying $20 an hour to learn to fly the Jenny. Later, after buying three planes, he opened a flying school in Modesto.

After being hired by movie stunt pilot Paul Mantz to teach at the Goddard Flying School in Palo Alto, he met Phyllis Innes Goddard, wife of the school's owner. Phyllis, a licensed pilot who also did stunt flying, was a charter member of the "Cloud Nine," a women's flying group.

Phyllis, who was born on the island of Elba, had come to the United States by way of British Columbia, where she had been staying with relatives.

Shortly after Penfield began working at the flying school, Norman Goddard, Phyllis' husband, was killed while stunt flying at a local air show.

By the time Penfield arrived in Santa Maria to join the other notable instructors, he and Phyllis were already married.

After war was declared, the sleepy rural airport became a bed of activity as young cadets went through their ten-week basic training at the school.

When the Penfields arrived in Santa Maria, Phyllis put her flying days behind her and became active in church affairs by playing the organ at St. Peter's Episcopal Church and directing the children's choir. This elegant woman was also a gifted artist, and when the church decided to change its entrance, it used sketches submitted by Phyllis to design the new entrance.

Phyllis Penfield was considered by many to be the "lifeblood of the church." Parishioners often said, "If it's okay with Phyllis, the Bishop will surely approve." This many-talented woman also served as secretary to Cap Twitchell for many years. After she passed away in 1984 and her ashes were sent to Victoria, B.C., a stained glass window depicting St. Cecelia was placed in St. Peter's and dedicated to Phyllis Penfield, the organist who had served the church for so many years.

The Penfields had no children and lived a simple, quiet life together. They enjoyed classical music and were both members of the Symphony Society.

When the contract with the government ended and Hancock's flying school disbanded in 1944, Tom became the personal pilot for Captain Hancock, a job that he held until Capt. Hancock passed away in May of 1965.

In addition to his lifelong interest in aviation, Tom Penfield, a tall, slender and quiet man, also spent a great deal of time shooting at the rifle range, using ammunition that he'd made in his workshop.

After Tom passed away at 95 years of age in February of 1993, his ashes were sent to Victoria to be buried alongside his wife of so many years.

Santa Marians Go to War

HEN THE CRISIS IN EUROPE, which had been building up since the signing of the Armistice in 1918, finally broke out in an all-out war in September of 1939, the entire continent was thrown into a state of disorder.

Fourteen months later, the United States instituted the first peacetime draft in its history, and the Selective Service began to call up the country's young men to help strengthen its defenses and to warn the warring factions across the Atlantic that the United States would fight to maintain its neutrality.

Still, though, Hitler continued to storm Europe, and the dark clouds of war over the Pacific skies were growing darker and darker as the Japanese continued to provoke the United States at every turn.

The Hancock College of Aeronautics, which had opened its doors in 1929, began to provide 10-week training classes as a contract school for the Army Air Corps in 1940, a school that was destined to become one of the most important flight training schools in the country.

However, the country was still reeling from the effects of the Great Depression, and even though the economy was greatly improved and the New Deal created jobs and restored dignity to millions of Americans, vast numbers of unemployed men were still walking the streets.

With the building of Camp Roberts and Camp San Luis Obispo, thousands of men flocked to the West Coast in search of work.

When the draft was instituted, thousands of young men left their homes to serve 365 days in military service, feeling that, if this action would keep us out of another war, it was well worth the sacrifice. These men would serve as needed, until the emergency was over.

"Be back in a year," the men hollered as they boarded the buses that would take them to various military installations for training.

George Scott, who headed the draft board in Santa Maria, made it a point throughout his service with the board to be at the bus stop to see the men off.

For the most part, draftees considered their service as just something that needed to be done. Hundreds of thousands of young men followed their consciences, donned khaki uniforms and waited for their one year of service to come to an end so that they could return home and get on with life. A hitch in the Army would bring in a bit of money and give hope that when they'd served their time and maybe learned a trade, jobs might be waiting for them when they returned.

When Stanley Muñoz received a letter from George Scott in November of 1940, giving him the chance to get in before the first inductees, he became the first and only Santa Marian to enlist on that day. After a big party given in his honor at the Elks Club, he went to Fort MacArthur, where he stayed two days before being transferred to Wyoming for six months.

Muñoz eventually wound up in New Guinea, where he spent the remaining war years before finally coming home in June of 1945, after having served a few months short of five years.

In September of 1941, though, when the 365 day-draftees saw that the government was moving closer to war in Europe and they knew that their one-year hitch would be extended, they began using the code "OHIO," an acronym for "Over the hill in October."

Many Santa Marians had already joined the Army Air Corps long before the draft. Bob Rivers joined in December of 1939 and received his flight training at Parks Air College in East St. Louis, Illinois.

Smokey Silva, who graduated from Santa Maria High School in 1939, received a letter from the local draft board advising him that if he were not in the service before January of 1942, he'd be drafted.

Silva joined the Army Air Force three days before the bombing of Pearl Harbor. He spent four years as a gunner with the 487th bomb group, making a total of 34 missions before the war finally ended and he returned to resume life in Santa Maria.

Smokey Silva served as a gunner during World War II

During the World War II period, 8 million men and women were serving in the Army, which at that time included the Air Corps. When the war ended, the Army was reduced by 6 million.

While many young men had made the supreme sacrifice and never returned, and many returned wearing the scars of the battle, the war was over, and hearts were filled with fervent hopes that it would never happen again.

Trelauney, the Tennessee Walker

HE COST OF WAGING THE WAR was staggering in both blood and money. America was "right smack in the middle of the biggest, deadliest, dirtiest war" in its history.

War bond drives to help offset the costs of fighting World War II began in November of 1942, and by the time the war ended in 1945, eight different bond drives had brought in $227 billion to help offset the direct military cost of the war. This single achievement has never been matched before or since.

In 1943, when the Allied forces were finally on the offensive on both fronts, Americans became optimistic. However, the war wasn't over yet.

On August 4, 1943, at a War Bond drive held the Veterans Memorial Building, Mrs. Leona Pearl Haslam of Santa Maria acquired Colonel Manning's Tennessee Walking Filly in return for her $25,000 bond pledge.

Later, when Mrs. Haslam saw her feed bills getting out of hand and she wanted to get rid of the horse, the Santa Maria B.P.O.E. #1538 stepped in and became the proud owners of "Trelauney," the Tennessee Walker.

The Elks Recreation Foundation, formed on November 18, 1943, organized a dance to be held the following December, and offered Trelauney as the door prize. The dance was a rousing success, with the Elks netting $1,177 and Leo Scaroni winning the coveted prize. Scaroni eventually gave the filly to his son-in-law, Frank Harrington of San Luis Obispo.

The lodge, with the exception of its financial officers, was happy with the profits gained from the dance. Although $1,177 was a tidy sum, it was too big to sit on and too little to do much with.

During a discussion of what to do with the money, the idea of a rodeo was first suggested. After consulting local rodeo experts and being assured that the costs of putting on such an event would not exceed $3,000, the club voted to underwrite the first annual Elks Recreation Foundation Benefit Wild West Show and Race Meet at a cost "not to exceed $3,000."

Although the show was a success, it didn't go without mishap. Russ Griffith, Past Exalted Ruler and first rodeo general chairman, recalled: "Two bulls broke out and ran around the fairgrounds. It seemed people were jammed around that arena 10 feet deep. We were just plain lucky, as we didn't have a dime's worth of insurance. Anyhow, we went ahead in pure ignorance and when the chips were through, the rodeo had cost $9,900, but we showed a $3,000 profit."

Each day of this two-day event began with a mounted horse parade starting from the Veteran's Memorial Building and ending at the Fairgrounds.

Horseracing, at that time, was a part of the rodeo and paid more than bull-riding and other events. However, in 1964, when the state decided to replace the racetrack at the fairgrounds with exhibit buildings, fairground horse racing came to an end. With the rodeo being such a success, the next problem facing the organization was what to do with the money.

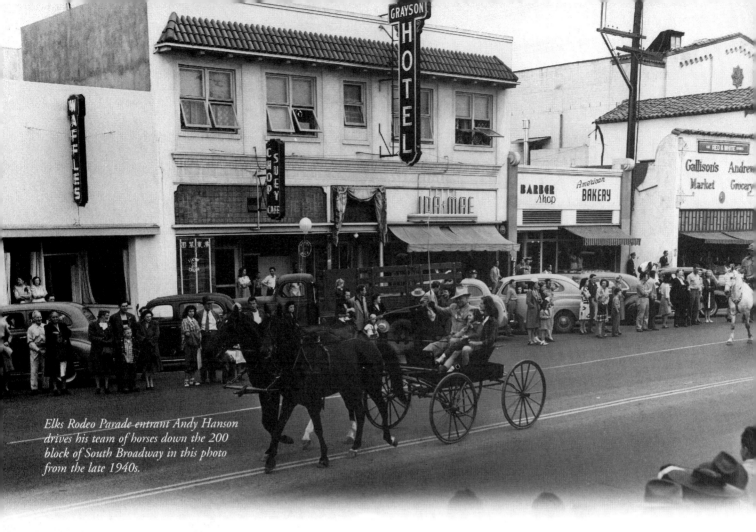

Elks Rodeo Parade entrant Andy Hanson drives his team of horses down the 200 block of South Broadway in this photo from the late 1940s.

When the group decided to gear the profits towards local recreation programs, young people benefited. Organizations having their start or encouragement from the Elks Recreation Foundation include Little League; the Santa Maria Indians (a top semi-pro baseball organization); Biddy Basketball; Swim to Live; 4-H; Future Farmers of America; Camp Fire Girls; the annual Christmas Parade, plus many other youth-oriented groups.

As the years passed and the Rodeo grew in stature, so did the quality of performances. The names of some of the contestants have appeared in the Cowboy Hall of Fame.

However, the rodeo didn't go without mishap. In 1949, Carl Engel, one of the rodeo's founders, was thrown over a fence during a mule race, and in 1963, Bobby Clark, the rodeo clown, was knocked unconscious by a bull.

During the 1970s, when Clarence Minetti, owner of the Far Western Tavern (and long-time active Elk member), herded the longhorn cattle from his Los Corralitos Ranch near Guadalupe down the Broadway parade route, Santa Maria police chief Richard Long looked a bit skeptical and said, "I sure hope you know what you're doing."

Not only is the Elks Rodeo one of the top attractions in the west and the third largest rodeo within the state, it was at one time among the top 25 sanctioned Professional Rodeo Cowboys Association events in the country.

Since the first rodeo, when the Elks netted a modest $3,000 profit, the community has looked at this annual event with pride, knowing that millions of dollars raised during the years have gone to programs that aid the youth of the area.

However, the annual Santa Maria Elks Rodeo and Parade might never have come about if it had not been for a horse by the name of "Trelauney," a horse that no one wanted.

The McGinley Family

PHOTOS COURTESY OF ANN COONERTY.

The McGinley family. Standing, left to right: Dad Neil, Ray, Joe, Mom Rose, Ann.
Kneeling: Connie (John C.), Larry, Jimmy.

Lawrence in 1922 and Jimmy, the youngest, came along in 1924. All of the McGinley children attended Orcutt Elementary School (the only school in Orcutt until after World War II), and later graduated from Santa Maria High School, where they not only excelled in sports, but were also active in school politics.

After high school, Francis obtained a football scholarship to the University of Southern California and became "all-time letterman" on the school's football team during the years of 1931 through 1933. After graduating from this prestigious university, he worked as a welder for Victory Welding, a position that was destined to keep him out of the war, as it was considered to be a job vital to the country's defense. He later worked for the Los Angeles Athletic Club, a job that he held until he retired.

When Connie graduated from high school in 1929, the country was in the midst of the Great Depression, and there just wasn't enough money to send him to college. To help support the family he joined his father in working in the oil fields.

Ann McGinley, editor of the *Review* in her senior year in high school, graduated in 1930 and

HILE ALL OF THE McGINLEY children were born in Lompoc, they grew up the Santa Maria Valley and attended local schools. Three brothers went off to war, and two never returned.

When Rose and Neil McGinley arrived in Lompoc from Donegal, Ireland (by way of Philadelphia), they lived on a farm in Lompoc until Neil obtained a job as a "pumper" in the oil fields of Union Oil and took his family to live on the Newlove lease.

Francis and John Cornelius "Connie" were tots and Ann was an infant when the "War to End All Wars" broke out in Europe in 1914. Joe was born in 1916, William Ray was born in 1920, enrolled in the University of California at Berkeley. Upon graduation in 1934, she taught at the Orcutt Elementary School for six years before marrying Kevin Coonerty, who served in an amphibious command in New Guinea for three years during World War II. After the war ended, the Coonertys moved to the Santa Cruz area, where Ann continued teaching until she retired from the school district. She later became a private tutor.

Ray McGinley graduated with the class of 1937, attended Santa Maria Junior College and later enlisted in the Army Air Corps, where he took cadet training.

After graduating from high school, Larry tried to get into aviation training, but since his eyesight wasn't perfect, he wasn't accepted. He later joined the Army and worked as a mechanic with a bomber squadron in England.

Jimmy, who graduated from high school in 1940, was the doctor of the family. After graduating from Berkeley and taking his internship in San Francisco, he enlisted in the Navy and served as a Navy doctor in Ohio.

The war years were tense times for the McGinley family, as they were for everyone who had a son, brother, husband or sweetheart serving in the war-torn countries.

The letter that the McGinleys received from Ray describing "Berlin in flames" proved to be his last communication.

In early April of 1944, the McGinleys received a telegram from the War Department reporting that their son was missing in action.

A second telegram, arriving shortly afterwards, advised that First Lieutenant William Ray McGinley, flying a P51 through heavy fog, had been killed in a plane collision somewhere over the British Channel.

Connie McGinley, who left the oil fields in March of 1942 when he received official notice from the draft board, took his training

with the 975th Field Artillery Battalion at Camp Forrest and left for overseas duty in February of 1944. His last letter home told of his being in Strasbourg. Larry, who had been serving in England for 15 months, had arranged for the two to get together in England. However, the brothers' planned reunion never took place, as Connie was alerted to go into battle.

Corporal John Cornelius McGinley was killed on January 11, 1945, in a gun explosion. His remains are buried in a military cemetery in Belgium, where local families attend the graves of United States servicemen who were killed in action. The body of Ray McGinley has never been recovered.

The two citations commemorating the death of the brothers, signed by Franklin Delano Roosevelt, are displayed on a wall at the Veterans of Foreign Wars building in Santa Maria, a post named after the McGinley brothers. Their purple hearts remain with the family.

Rose McGinley, who had been named Santa Maria's outstanding mother in 1948, passed away in 1965, and Neil died two years later. Both are buried in the Catholic Cemetery in San Fernando. 🌸

Rose McGinley remembers her sons who never came home from World War II.

Santa Maria During World War II

ALTHOUGH 1941 WASN'T a particularly good year for sports, with the Davis Cup and the Wimbledon matches being canceled because of the raging war in Europe, the hostilities in Europe didn't affect the World Series games.

On December 7, 1941, an unusually warm Sunday morning, the Reverend Bussingham, of St. Peter's Episcopal Church in Santa Maria, was preaching his sermon when his deacon passed

A piece of field artillery, shown here in 1926, was for many years a fixture on the front lawn of the Carnegie Library on South Broadway in Santa Maria. It was melted down for scrap during World War II.

him a note. The Reverend quickly scanned the message and announced to a startled congregation that a report had just come in that Japanese forces were bombing Pearl Harbor. Although not all of his parishioners knew where Pearl Harbor was, they were stunned, confused, and anxious to get home to turn on their radios.

After war was officially declared by President Roosevelt the next day, the people of the Central Coast began to mobilize their efforts, with each person doing his or her part in protecting the country from a possible attack by an enemy from another shore. All amateur radio stations were ordered off the air by the government and all planes were grounded, except those used for national defense and regular airway companies.

Within a month, Japanese submarines were seen off the coastal areas. On December 23, the Union Oil Company's tanker *Montebello* was sunk just off the coast at Cambria. Although no one was killed in that attack, five crewmen were killed when the Richfield Oil tanker *Emideo* was shelled twenty-five miles off Cape Mendocino.

This was a time of fear, confusion, misinformation and tension. By the following March, there wasn't much happening on the Pacific War Front that provided any reassurance.

An airplane watch was set up on the corner of Main Street and Suey Road, on the Cossa property, with women taking turns watching for planes. If a plane was spotted, the women were instructed to turn in this vital information, complete with what kind of plane it was, how high it was flying, and so forth.

Because it was generally felt that the West Coast

would ultimately be subjected to a strong enemy attack, blackouts were ordered for all communities along the coast, and the Santa Maria Railroad had blackout shields installed over its locomotive headlights. Because "every light along the coast, which is visible at sea, must be quenched," motorists were told to drive with their parking lights on, and then only when necessary. Troops from Camp Cooke, Fort Ord and San Luis Obispo took up beach positions and placed poles resembling cannons in bunkers along the sand dunes in hopes of discouraging a Japanese land invasion.

Government officials took away Howard Stornetta's local rain reports, confident in knowing that no foreign country could get hold of them to learn how much rain fell in the area.

Housewives were asked to save cooking grease and turn it in to the local meat market, to flatten and save tin cans, and to re-tailor their clothes. Everyone pitched in to help in the war effort, with children saving foil from gum wrappers and collecting metals and rubber to turn into the schools.

People were paid one cent per pound for their old tires, rubber raincoats, old garden hoses, rubber shoes, bathing caps, and other rubber-based items that they turned into service stations. The government, in turn, reimbursed the station owners.

Nylon stockings, which had just come into use at the start of the war, became non-existent until the war was over. Instead, women wore silk or rayon stockings—when they could get them. Leg makeup became an alternative to stockings.

Sunday farmers throughout the country planted over 20 million Victory Gardens to supplement fresh vegetables and to can for the winter months.

Civilian car production ended in 1942, not to resume until 1945, and rationing began.

In November of 1942, rationing of gasoline began, with allotments being made on the basis of "need of effort." The average person was allotted four gallons per week with an "A" card. Business people could obtain more gas with a "B" card,

while "C" card holders, those essential to the war effort, could get all of the gas they needed.

There was much grumbling about the gas rationing, with each person feeling that he warranted the much-coveted "C" card. Appeals were presented to Myrton Purkiss, Chairman of the Rationing Board. He, in turn, turned them over to the appeals committee members, Frank Johnson, Mayor Marion Rice, L. T. Thompson and W. W. Stokes, leaving them to make the final decisions.

When total rationing began, people were issued rationing books for each member of the family by the OPA.

Although gas-rationing books were separate and could be kept in the car for convenience, the general ration books were usually kept in a safe place inside the house. Each general rationing book, containing both red and blue stamps, was imprinted with the person's full name, along with his or her height, weight, color of hair and eyes, age and sex. Stamps (along with money, or course) were needed to buy sugar—when they could get it—and to buy shoes, with a limit of two pairs a year. However, shoes made of cloth with soles of rope didn't require stamps. "But boy, were they ever slick!"

Meat stamps, tire stamps, gas stamps, and butter stamps had people coveting their little rationing books. When a baby was born, no matter what time of the year he or she came into the world, a stamp book was issued.

Rationing books were not to be transferred and were to be surrendered in case of death or if a person left the country. Any person finding a lost book was required to turn it into the nearest Rationing Board.

When gasoline rationing ended in August of 1945, photos of people tearing up their rationing books appeared on the front pages of newspapers throughout the country. Butter rationing ended in 1944, tire rationing ended in December of 1945, but sugar rationing didn't end until June of 1947. ☙

Plane Crash on South Broadway!

URING WORLD WAR II, the Lockheed P-38 plane could fly further than most planes, and could carry more than twice as many bombs per flight than any other fighter plane. A close second was the British Mosquito, followed by the Tempest, the American F-44 Corsair and the P-47 Thunderbolt. Head-on attacks by the P-38s were especially fearsome. P-38s were known to return home from battle with their entire propellers smashed off and engines dangling. Nevertheless, they came home. Yes, the Lockheed P-38 plane was the best fighter plane of its day.

In early 1942, the Army Corps of Engineers started buying Santa Maria land just north of Orcutt to use as a B-25 base, and by May of that same year, 20 buildings and 3 runways had been built. On September 16, 1943, the Santa Maria Air Base became a training base for P-38 pilots.

With three major Army training bases and three military air bases located within a 50-mile radius of the town, Santa Marians soon became accustomed to the presence of the thousands of military personnel stationed in the area, and airplane formations in the open skies soon lost their novelty.

However, even though the valley prospered by

the influx of servicemen into the area, its people had doubts about the expertise of the pilots who were flying their sophisticated planes over the valley. Farmers and dairymen soon began to resent the ear-shattering routine training flights, and plane crashes became more frequent in number.

On Tuesday, January 30, 1945, with the country still fighting a war on both the European and Pacific fronts, local farmers looked with anticipation at the dark rain clouds which had formed over the area, as their fields were in dire need of a little moisture. By noon, though, the gray skies had lifted.

When twenty-one-year-old Flight Officer Elmer Steffy's plane lifted off the runway at about 12:30 in the afternoon and proceeded to take part in a normal two-formation, one-engine routine, this exercise would prove to be his last.

During this practice formation, Steffy's plane went into a deadly flat spin, and while Santa Marians watched in horror, the plane came crashing down right in the middle of Broadway, tearing off the roof of the Economy Drug Store and smashing into the wall of Rusconi's Café.

The plane's fireball of exploding gas blasted out Rusconi's front window, blowing Filippo Rusconi through the gaping hole. Mrs. Rusconi and the cook, John Doff, as well as pilot Steffy, were killed instantly.

Sandy Nicolai and her mother, who were eating lunch at the B & B Café across the street, were two of the many shocked townspeople who rushed to the scene. Fire Chief Crakes and his crew of mostly volunteer firemen, along with fire trucks from the airbase, were able to confine the blaze to the café, thus saving the Economy Drug

Store next door and other businesses in the area.

The crashing plane had cut the main power lines and the city was plunged into darkness.

When an assessment was made of the total damage, the Bradley Hotel, located across the alley from the crash, and the Economy Drug Store were found to have suffered minor damage. By nightfall, the scorched remains of the plane had been hauled away by truck.

The townspeople were outraged when, on the same day, another P-38 crashed near the Orcutt area, killing yet another pilot.

The city fathers asked why, with all of the vacant land located in the general area and the entire ocean to the west, was it necessary to prac-

tice war games over populated areas? Addressing the townspeople's concerns and offering sincere regrets, the commanding officer of the air base summoned the city's officials together and advised them that he'd issued a new order to his pilots. There would be no more flying at any altitude over the city of Santa Maria. 🦢

The Santa Maria Redskins

FTER WORLD WAR II ENDED and returning veterans were trying to pick up the pieces of lives, many of the men who had been active in high school sports often hung out in Big Boy Holman's store on North Broadway and talked about getting back into sports. However, with no local team, their chances of ever playing in sports again didn't look promising.

In 1947, Jim Gamble contacted the Los Angeles Recreation Department to check on possible track meets. He learned that although Los Angeles did have an open track meet once a year, that year's race had already been held. "However, if you guys had a football team," he was told, "there are about 50 teams down here that are looking for games outside the Los Angeles leagues."

With Santa Maria having more than its share of outstanding football players who had played the sport in both high school and college, Jim didn't

have to look far to find players to form a team. He only needed to put out the word. By the first of July, fifty men were ready to sign up.

Around the 1st of July in 1947, a meeting was held at Tom Moore's Café after closing hours, and before the night had ended, a team was formed: a team that marked the beginning of the Santa Maria Valley Athletic Club. The next day Gamble ordered 50 uniforms from Holman's (incurring a bill that Gamble said took three years to pay).

Jim Gamble was elected president of the team and soon became general manager, a position that he held until the club disbanded. Other officers included Gordon Taylor as vice president, and George Gallison, as secretary-treasurer, with Bill Massa and Dewitt Hogle on the finance committee.

Officials included Frank Holt, Ed Jorgensen, Nello Dal Porto, Al Maguire and Leroy Macdonald. Two of the club's earliest sponsors were G&O Productions (Goodman & Openshaw) and Myrtle and R.H. Tesene's Beacon Outpost.

The game, like today, was rough. However, unlike today, football helmets didn't have any nose guards, and injuries were commonplace. Still, though, the men gave the game everything they had, and some of their experiences are still spoken of in wonder—sometimes the wonder of having survived.

Before the first game was even played, fullback Wilbert Grabil was seriously injured during a scrimmage and spent the rest of the season recuperating.

None of the games went without mishap. Before the team played its first game in Santa Cruz, Irene Engle and Barbara Walters drove off with the team's football helmets in the trunk of the car. The game was delayed while players and the Santa Cruz police searched for the ladies.

During that Santa Cruz game, Buddy Villa, the team's first string halfback who had just carried the ball over the goal line to score the Redskins' first touchdown, broke his arm and was out for the rest of the season.

The following week, four players were seriously injured in an automobile accident while on their way down to play a game in San Pedro. The 1947 season ended early because of the death of Stanley (Marty) Martinez, the team's head coach.

Although the season was over, a team from Hemet, the Tahquetz Packers, called Gamble and offered to pay extra money if the Redskins would fill in for another team that had backed out of a Thanksgiving game with them. The Hemet team was in a bind. All of the tickets had been sold, and issuing a refund to 2400 fans was out of the question.

Gamble was able to round up twenty-four men who were willing to forego Thanksgiving dinner and go down to Hemet.

When the Santa Maria team arrived at the field and began to dress for the game, it was discovered that instead of twenty-four players, only twelve had shown up—and one those twelve was subject to muscle spasms.

George Gallison, who had come along to fill in for manager Dick Trefts, was suited up and quickly went from manager to player. When the father-in-law of another player was suited up, the Santa Maria Redskins had a baker's dozen, and was ready to go.

History was made that day when Gallison, who had never played in a game before, caught a 35-yard pass in the end zone to tie the game. When Frankie Reis kicked the extra point, the Redskins won the game 7 to 6.

On the way home, Gallison bought dinner for everyone. The hero of the day never played football again.

In 1948, Santa Maria's mayor, Glen Seaman, was able to secure a football field for the men next to the Elks baseball field along Miller Street. The first home game was played against the Santa Barbara College Junior Varsity. However, since the open field permitted spectators to watch the game without paying, and the club wasn't making any money, the team decided to play its home games in the Santa Maria High School field.

The Redskins played against any team that wanted to play football. Just before the team's first game against the Lompoc Penitentiary began, a crowd of inmates came tearing across the field yelling like a bunch of savages. The Santa Maria team breathed a sigh of relief after realizing that there were more spectators than there were seats in the bleachers. It was simply a case of "every man for himself." That particular game went on and on until darkness fell and the prison officials finally came out to call the game, as the prisoners had to be in before dark.

There was a lot of camaraderie among the men and a lot of just plain hard-nosed football. They played for the love of the sport and had a good time, win or lose.

By the time Santa Maria's semi-professional football team disbanded in 1953, the Redskins had won 30 games, lost 30 and tied two.

Lester Hayes

N 1921, WHEN SILENT MOVIES were the rage and Harry Dorsey needed an organist at his Gaiety Theatre on East Main Street, he offered the job to Frank Hayes, then a noted organist at the Golden Gate Theater in San Francisco.

When the Hayes family stepped off the trolley in Santa Maria, having just come into town from the Guadalupe train depot, young Lester saw Herb Swanson leading a group of musicians performing in front of the old Bradley Hotel.

Hayes' career was destined to last only six years. In 1927, when the innovative Movie Tone came out with the first talking movie, *The Jazz Singer,* all theater organists were put out of business, and Frank needed a new job.

Seeing a need in the local schools, Frank Hayes went to Sacramento to take a test to give him the proper credentials with which to teach music in the public schools. Although music had long been taught in the schools back east, the Santa Maria schools had never considered the subject important enough to be included in the schools' curriculum. After Hayes convinced the districts that music was essential to a child's growth, and the schools began a music program, he became the first Director of Instrumental Music in the Santa

Maria Elementary School District. He eventually brought the area's school program on an even par with those of the eastern states.

Lester Hayes' professional music career began at the age of sixteen, when he joined a band sponsored jointly by the American Legion and the City of Santa Maria. Phil Broshe, a local insurance salesman, both played the trumpet and served as the band's leader. Lester, who played the clarinet, later served as the band's leader for eight years.

For many years the American Legion/City Band was the only band that marched in the local parades. The band members would lead the parade to the end of the parade route and then jump aboard a waiting truck and be driven back to the starting line where they would begin marching the parade route once again.

After Lester graduated from San Jose State in 1934, he had problems in trying to keep the band together, as there just weren't enough old-timers around any more. Although he used high school music students to fill in when necessary, his problems increased when the older members and the students couldn't seem to get along.

Lester, a charter member of the Santa Maria Symphony Orchestra, played with the Hancock Ensemble while attending Santa Maria Junior

In this undated scene from the 1940s, Lester Hayes (center, dark suit) pauses for a photo while rehearsing with his elementary school orchestra.

College. In 1926 he became a member of the Community Orchestra, a musical group directed by the renowned musician from the Los Angeles area, William Edson Strobridge.

The first youth band, made up of junior high school students, was formed by Frank Hayes and sponsored by the Elks Lodge. The members wore white uniforms supplied by the Elks. By the time that Lester became the band's director, the uniform's colors had changed from all white to blue and white.

When Frank Hayes passed away, Lester, who had been studying for his M.A. degree at Berkeley, came home to take his father's place as music director in the school district. After Lester retired in 1971, both the Elks Band and the American Legion/City Band dissolved.

Throughout his life Lester Hayes was involved in every aspect of music in the Santa Maria Valley. In addition to his being a charter member of the Santa Maria Symphony Orchestra and a founding member and director of the Harmony Club, he taught and directed instrumental music in Santa Maria, Guadalupe, Orcutt and Sisquoc. He spent two years teaching orchestral music at his alma mater, Santa Maria High School. Always interested in young people, Hayes began a music program for the city's youngsters, offering music instruction at to charge. The recreational games that he organized for his music students became such a success that the city of Santa Maria assumed the program and formed the Santa Maria Recreation Department.

Known as "Mr. Band," Lester Hayes took his

bands to compete in other towns and cities. In addition to marching in the Salinas and Santa Barbara Christmas parades for many years, they also marched in Disneyland.

The respect and admiration for Lester Hayes knew no bounds. Some of his former music students went on to greater positions in the field of music, with one serving as the head of the music department at a University in Hawaii. Truman Fisher became the head of the music department at Cal State, Irvine, and Joe Fuller played with the Dukes of Dixieland.

Unknown to many people, Hayes' early ambitions in life didn't include music. "I didn't want to be a musician," he once confessed. "I wanted to be involved in athletics. But when Friday and Saturday came along, I played in a nightclub, because I had to earn money." Since teams travel on weekends, he by necessity chose music.

Following his retirement in 1971, Hayes took up woodcarving, a hobby that soon won him awards as being tops in his field.

In July of 1999, Hayes was one of three recipient of the first Meritorious Community Service Awards given to three long-time community leaders and volunteers who were recognized as having made significant contributions "impacting Santa Maria's leisure lifestyle." The following year he was awarded a Meritorious Community Service Award by the Santa Maria Recreation and Parks Commission in recognition of his many contributions and efforts on behalf of the youth of the city.

Lester Hayes, Santa Maria's "Mr. Band," passed away on the 13th of September in 1999, at ninety years of age. ❧

Elwin Mussell and Mussell Fort

LWIN MUSSELL, A NATIVE OF South Dakota, came to Santa Maria with his family when he was a 16-year-old boy. Without much in the way of education but loaded with determination, he took a correspondence course, learned the printing trade, and proceeded to become a "self-made man."

Advertising supported Mussell's *Santa Maria Advertiser,* a free newspaper "independent as a hog on ice." The newspaper, published every Thursday, contained editorials as well as advertising.

In 1944 Mussell purchased 160 acres in Ruiz Canyon from the attorney, Fred Gobel. Additional land purchases of adjoining property increased the man's land ownership in the area to almost 574 acres.

An avid Democrat, Mussell served on Santa Maria's City Council for eight years and as Mayor from 1974 to 1980. During his term in office plans were formulated to build the Town Center Mall, the first mall in town.

Elwin Mussell's idea in building Mussell Fort, which he began building in 1952, was to use it as his own personal showplace as well as to show it off to friends.

Although a forest fire in 1953 destroyed some of the property at the fort, the kitchen, with its green redwood, was only slightly scorched.

Mussell Fort, built on two of his 574 acres, had seven buildings, two of which came from Santa Maria. "Audrey's Alcove," the tallest of the buildings, formerly sat on a used car lot on West Main Street. Another building, in order to be moved, had to be cut in many sections and reassembled when it reached its destination. It had formerly been a cat house (a building used to raise cats).

The Room and Board House, the Saloon—complete with swinging doors—the Sheriff's office and even the general merchandise store, with its carved wooden Indians, made this little fort in the mountains one of California's best-kept secrets.

Always looking for something that would fit into his fort, Mussell traveled to 47 states, picking up such items as branding irons, brass knuckles, handcuffs, a whaling kettle, buckboards, a six-sided poker table, and items from the first grocery store in Morro Bay.

The electric generator from the late 1800s had been used for gold plating by Alfred Lutnetsky, a Santa Maria jeweler.

A piece of field artillery, which had once stood in front of the Veteran's Memorial Building, was col-

PHOTO COURTESY OF AUDREY AND DOUGLAS MUSSELL

lected by the federal government in a scrap metal drive during World War II. After the war ended, the government gave the city a piece of Japanese artillery, but since the city didn't want it, the weapon was placed in a junkyard, where it sat for seven years. With the city's permission, Mussell hauled it up to the fort, where he added it to his collection.

The second of Mussell's weapon pieces was one made in France in 1874 and built for use in chasing Indians. However, the weapon was in mint condition, as it had never been used. The barrels of both weapons were welded shut and served only as points of interest.

The unofficial landmark known as Mussell's

Mussell Fort, 1996

Fort and located about 20 miles from Santa Maria, was a step back in time.

The signed photos of Franklin Delano Roosevelt that adorned the walls brought back memories of Mussell's active campaigning on behalf of the president.

The signed card from "Death Valley Shorty" was definitely one of a kind. The six streetlights that once lit the streets of Santa Maria, five of them in working condition, kept Mussell Fort well lit.

In May of 1980, on his way home to Santa Maria from his fort, Elwin Mussell died in a car accident. His wife, Barbara, who suffered from an extended illness, died 11 days later.

145

Eugene Lenz

HE XVII OLYMPIAD opened on August 25, 1960, with much pomp and ceremony, as the President of Italy declared the games open at 8:30 a.m. (PDT). Although it was a sweltering day, over 90,000 spectators were jammed into the white concrete Olympic Stadium, ready to watch the world's finest amateur athletes compete against each other for the much coveted gold, silver and bronze medals.

As helicopters hovered overhead, a glittering parade of contestants from eighty-five competing nations took part in the opening ceremony. The United States delegation of 200 men and women wore uniforms of blue and white, with the men wearing white straw hats banded with red, white and blue.

One of the U.S.A. team members was Eugene Lenz, son of Adolph and Marian Lenz of Santa Maria. Gene had been swimming for as long as he could remember. Born in San Luis Obispo, he was a year old

when he came with his family to the $5000 house that his father, a long-time Union Oil man, had built at 909 Haslam Drive. Along with his brother Leonard and sister Nadine, Gene went through the Santa Maria school system, passing through Miller Street School—where his mother taught for many years—El Camino Junior High School, and finally Santa Maria High School, where he graduated with the class of 1955.

As a freshman at the high school, Gene was encouraged by Paul Nelson of the Santa Maria Plunge to try out for the high school's swimming team. When Phil Wahl, the high school's swimming coach, pulled him aside and advised, "You ought to be in competitive swimming," the boy began a four-year period of serious swimming competition during which he represented the school in various meets throughout the state.

After graduating from Santa Maria High School in 1955, Lenz enrolled in Cal Poly on a work scholarship, where he majored in Architectural Engineering.

By his second year at the San Luis Obispo university, Lenz had

re-written all school records. Richard Anderson, Cal Poly swimming coach, was so impressed with the young man that he arranged for him to go to Yale University during the summer to practice under Robert Kiputh, one of the greatest swimming coaches in the country. The four summers that he worked under Kiputh paid off: in ACC swimming championships in his Senior year, he placed third in the 1500-meter freestyle and fourth in the 400-meter freestyle.

Year after year Lenz was one of the top winners at the National AAU and the NCAA Swim finals. In 1959, during his fourth year at Cal Poly, he placed third in the 1500-meter and the 400-meter freestyle trials held up in the Bay area, thus earning a place on a team of top U. S. swimmers slated to tour Japan. A week after the trials, the team flew to Japan and spent three weeks in competition against teams in Tokyo, Osaka, Nagasaki, and Hiroshima.

After returning from Japan, Lenz flew to Indianapolis, where he became one of the three top men in still another event, making him eligible to go to the Pan American games in Chicago later that summer. Americans took the first three places in the 400-meter freestyle at the Chicago games, with Lenz placing third. Trials held during the following year determined which two swimmers in each event would be part of the Olympic team. At Detroit, Lenz placed second in the 400-meter freestyle and was awarded a berth on the United States Olympic team.

However, it wasn't over yet. After flying to Rome, the young men competed again in preliminaries to determine the top eight contestants for the Olympic finals in each event. On August 30, Lenz swam his way into the finals of the 400-meter freestyle event.

In talking about life in the Olympic contest, where the best athletes in the world competed against each other, Lenz said that his team was very close-knit. "We ate together, swam together and saw Rome together," he remembered. "We were quartered, living two in a room, and ate steak two times a day."

In the final competition, Lenz finished seventh and timed in at 4:26.8, about three seconds faster than his qualifying time. Murray Rose of Australia, who won the gold medal, timed in at 4:18.3.

With the stress of Olympic competition behind them, the American teams began touring different parts of Italy, meeting amateur swimmers and playing polo with a team in the northern part of the country. When Lenz finally arrived home on September 14, his parents, along with a reporter from the *Santa Maria Times,* were there to meet him at the Santa Maria Airport.

For Lenz, swimming competition ended as he pursued his education. After graduating from Cal Poly in 1960 with a degree in Structural Engineering, he joined the Navy, where he remained for ten years, completing three tours of duty in Vietnam. After his discharge he returned to Santa Maria, where he took a job with Fluor Engineering.

Eugene Lenz was Santa Maria's second swimmer to go to the Olympics. John Paulsen had represented the United States in the 1932 Olympiad competition in Los Angeles.

At one time, Lenz held fourteen school records. He was Cal Poly's first All-American Swimmer and won the California State College swimming championship in three different events in four years. He was inducted into the University's Hall of Fame in 1987.

The Santa Maria Valley Historical Society

URING THE EARLY 1950s, a group of concerned townspeople, spearheaded by Ethel-May Dorsey, was concerned that the history of the town would be lost with the passing of its pioneers. It began a project of recording conversations with some of the people whose families had been the earliest settlers in the valley. When the project met with enthusiasm, the idea of forming a historical society took root.

On September 7, 1955, during the 50th anniversary celebration of the incorporation of the city of Santa Maria, the Santa Maria Valley Historical Society was organized and incorporated as a non-profit organization, with Ethel-May Dorsey serving as its first president. Over 200 people signed up as charter members.

As donations of various artifacts were received by the organization, it needed a place in which to store them. The city permitted the group to use the basement of the Carnegie Library, but when dampness threatened to damage the historical treasures, the society began to look for other sites.

Although the museum was to know a number of homes during the next ten years, the need for a permanent museum site was apparent.

In 1959, when the book *This Is Our Valley* was published, the group's treasury grew.

Ted Bianchi, who took over the presidency of the Historical Society in 1971, spearheaded plans to build a permanent museum. When children in the local schools joined the campaign and collected $1200 in pennies, nickels and dimes, their efforts instigated a fund-raising campaign such as the city had never seen before. The valley wanted and needed a historical museum, and the townspeople were determined that it was going to have one.

In the fall of 1973, construction began on the building. Through the efforts of many, the fully paid-for building located on city property was dedicated on January 20, 1974. The building, housing both the Santa Maria Valley Historical Museum and the Santa Maria Chamber of Commerce offices, is located in the 600 block of South Broadway.

The building of the Santa Maria Valley Historical Museum became the pride of the city and was met with total community support. It continues to be a vibrant organization dedicated to preserving the history of the Santa Maria Valley.

Index